Also by L. E. Hewitt

Life Between the Raindrops
My Wonderful Chaos
Chasing the Silver Lining
My Bucket List Has a Hole in It

I Don't Have A Button for That

L.E. HEWITT

SEABOARD PRESS

JAMES A. ROCK & COMPANY, PUBLISHERS

I Don't Have A Button for That by L. E. Hewitt

SEABOARD PRESS

is an imprint of JAMES A. ROCK & CO., PUBLISHERS

I Don't Have A Button for That copyright ©2015 by L.E. Hewitt

Special contents of this edition copyright ©2015 by Seaboard Press

Address comments and inquiries to:
SEABOARD PRESS
1937 West Palmetto Street, #6
Florence, South Carolina 29501

E-mail:
jrock@rockpublishing.com   lrock@rockpublishing.com
Internet URL: www.rockpublishing.com

Trade Paperback ISBN: 978-1-59663-876-1

Printed in the United States of America

First Edition: 2015

*Interested readers may
wish to visit the author's website:*

www.lehewitt.net

*This book
is dedicated to
Kevin and Julie*

*my lifelong
friends*

Contents

Foreword

Living is a continual series of changes. Many you can antici-
pate, while most just smack you in the face unexpectedly. This is
often not a bad thing, although we may frequently believe so at
the time. Typically, these changes open doors to new adventures
and great opportunities. The key is attitude. Just put on your
blinders and keep doing what your heart tells you to do and you
will be just fine.

One of the biggest changes I have faced in recent times is the
growing up of my children. I did not realize how much I would
miss being needed on a daily basis. I miss having those lunkheads
around for me to solve their problems! Shelly, Elizabeth and Will
have all grown into responsible young adults. I cannot take the
credit for that. I just got lucky to have great kids.

This newfound singularity in which I live has opened up op-
tions for me to do some other things I always wanted. I am even
able to write full time now. That part is a good thing. But honestly, I would give it all back for the kids to be little again. Don't
get me wrong, I keep smiling and am happy every day for my
blessed life. But, I would go back and try to be a better dad in a
heartbeat.

This book is a look at the lighter side of a great time of transi-
tion in my own life. I hope you enjoy *I Don't Have a Button for
That.*

Feeling Fowl

It has been an interesting weekend. The highlight/lowlight was a trip to WalMart. From the moment I walked into the place, nearly every woman there was staring at me. I mean, I know I look good, but dang! I was feeling quite the ladies' man until I remembered that I had eighteen multi-colored wires glued to my head and dangling down my back. All of those women were looking at me and wondering what was wrong with me! So much for my inflated ego!

The story begins way back in June. Back then I had a mild stroke. I have since healed wonderfully and those issues have gone away but the doctor wanted to redo the tests for comparison. One of those tests was a 72 hour EEG. They glue 18 wires to your head, connect them to a data recorder on your waist and say see you in three days. So, anyhow, here I have been all weekend, feeling fine but looking like I must be being kept alive by artificial means. People have been opening doors, letting me cut in front of them in lines. These are total strangers. The department store door greeter said she would pray for me. I cannot wait to go back there and proclaim that I am healed!

Today I finally get the wires removed. I am most looking forward to scratching my head for about an hour. It will be a glorious moment.

Forward to results day ... Back in the summer I had a health scare. I was told I had suffered a mild stroke. I had some odd tinglings for a while and I was a bit tired and such but I quickly recovered to feeling like myself again. During that time, the doctor ordered tons of tests checking me for all sorts of horrible stuff. Some of the tests came back showing some abnormalities. But, since I was improving, the doctor took a wait and see approach. About a month ago the doctor said that it was time to redo all of those tests for comparison purposes. So I spent many days recently being poked, prodded and even shocked. Well, Monday was my results day. The doctor walked in and proclaimed that all of my tests results had improved. During this week of Thanksgiving, I had been given something tangible to truly be thankful for ... Peace of mind. It is good to know that I am back to ... well, I guess I shouldn't say normal as I have never been normal in my life, but at least I am back to me.

For Thanksgiving Day, we went to my mother-in-law's house. I thought that was a good deal. You take an hour's drive, sit down and eat food which has already been prepared, loaf on the couch watching football for a while, then drive back home. No fuss, no mess, no cooking, no cleaning. The only problem is that Sally got home and realized that there were no leftovers. So what does she do? Well, she ran out to the store on Friday and bought a turkey and all of the fixin's and made a second Thanksgiving dinner just so she could have the leftovers. I think she has gone completely nuts. I thought I had avoided the worst part of Thanksgiving, eating turkey fourteen different ways until it is gone. Worst of all, I forgot to mention, she didn't just buy any old turkey. She bought a 21lb. turkey. It barely fit in the oven! If I am lucky, I will be done eating this one in time for Christmas, at which point Sally will make ANOTHER turkey. Somebody please help me!

Pause

Life needs a pause button. What I mean is that things get too busy and it would be nice to be able to take a break without missing anything. Just hit the Life Pause Button, go take a nap on a quiet beach for a month or two, then hit play again and get right back to living without missing anything. Wouldn't that be cool? Of course you would not be allowed to ponder or fret over things as that would defeat the purpose. Your job in Life Pause would simply be to relax and enjoy the peace.

Of course being the type of person that I am, I would also enjoy a Recreation Button. Like most people, I spend most of my life working and doing various chores. I would love to have a button that would give me six weeks of recreation. For me that would be things like Golf, Racquetball, Basketball, Horseshoes, Bocce Ball, Playing Music, Camping, Writing, Hiking, and a whole list of other activities. Why do I rarely get to do that stuff yet I get to do the not so fun stuff every day? Not Fair!

High School Concert

I went to a high school band "Holiday" Concert this evening. They don't call them Christmas shows anymore. I am fine with being inclusive to other holiday celebrations. Everybody has the right to choose their own path. It would be silly for someone to try and force their way of life on someone else. I know that some may try, but I believe that each person should be able to choose.

As for the concert, I enjoyed it immensely. Many people go just out of obligation to their kids, but I enjoy the music. The fact that I have a kid there performing just makes it even better. I have an appreciation for many types of music and I enjoy live shows so it all fits for me. I was sitting there tapping my feet and humming along perfectly content. For me things like this are a part of the good stuff in my life.

Fighting Fat

I love to wear shorts. I love to wear them so much that I am often the last person around to give in to long pants for the winter. That moment finally arrived one recent cold, blustery day. I reluctantly pulled out my jeans and put them on resigned to my fate, but wait, there seemed to be a large problem here. Over the summer this pair of pants had shrunk so severely that I could not begin to get them buttoned. Ok, no big deal, I had four or five more pairs in reserve. In succession I tried on each pair with the same result. My spirit was beginning to be shaken. I moved on to the three pairs of khakis. Same result! Surely Sally must have washed them wrong before they were put away for the summer. That, that mean evil woman! Or could it be, oh no, how could I dare even to think it! No way! So I pulled out the scales and stepped on them just to be on the safe side. Oh crap! I'm FAAAAAAAAAAAAAT! I had gained a good solid 15 pounds since last winter. How could this have happened? There had to be some mistake! No matter how hard I tried to find a reason, I had to face the fact that I have become a glutton and I needed to watch what I eat for a while. What a way to start the Christmas season!

Christmas Cookies

We have less than two weeks remaining until Christmas. The best part about that is that the cookies will be arriving soon. Mom may be 85 but she still ships the cookies every year. Admittedly the boxes have gotten a bit smaller and the variety may have diminished a bit, but those cookies still come! One day soon I will hear the mailman pull up and I will open that box sent straight from heaven filled with sugar, chocolate chip, orange iced, and potato chip cookies and maybe even nut rolls! Yes, there is such a thing as a potato chip cookie and it is one of my favorites. My mommy has made them for me every year for as long as I can remember. The sugar cookies are just a plain, old fashioned thick, soft cookie. Even the old dog looks forward to those ones. She will follow me around the house just to catch a crumb or two. I will have to hide the box from Sally and the kids or it will soon be nothing but a memory. Share? You think I should share? But my mommy loves ME the best I just know it! And don't tell her I am planning on keeping the cookies all for myself either!

The Mall at Christmas

I had to go to the mall for my daughter Shelly the other day. I cannot tell you why I had to go because somebody might read this and learn about their Christmas gift, but let's just say I had to go that day because Shelly was working. She goes to college but works part time on weekends. It was Saturday afternoon about 4pm when I went to the mall. Saturday December 17th. The last Saturday before Christmas. I must have been insane. The traffic was backed up for a mile before you got to the entrance. The traffic was backed up at the end of every parking aisle. There were 4000 cars looking for a parking space and about one parking space an hour being vacated. I finally gave up on finding my own space and just parked on top of a Mini Cooper.

Once inside the mall I had three goals I needed to accomplish. I have always been good at navigating a crowd so I had little fear that I could be in and out in no time at all. Did you know that grown women can growl and snarl at you if you pick up a scarf that they are considering buying a week before Christmas? Did you know that they will take you out below the knees if you cut in front of them in line? I was scared for my life in there! I grabbed what I needed as fast as I could and then ran for my life. I jumped into the car and backed out of my parking spot as quickly as I could and then I sat there and sat there and sat there for what seemed like hours. Getting out was worse than getting in. A trip that would normally take 20 minutes turned into a 3 hour adventure.

But now I am done with shopping and ready to sit back and relax while thinking about those poor other souls still stuck in traffic at the mall.

Christmas Cherished

Each and every Christmas season should be cherished. We only get a few of them in our lifetime. While we may not like the commercialization and the hype and materialism assigned to this season, on an individual basis, Christmas is what you choose to make it. Whether it is a time of spiritual renewal or reconnection with family or creating magic in the lives of children or lending a helping hand to those who could use one, this is the season to make great memories.

I personally have many great memories of this season. Several of them are just little things, but things that are embedded in my heart. I remember dad. He loved Christmas. He would string tinsel around every doorway in the house and from corner to corner across the living room ceiling. He would bounce around the house with renewed spirit singing "It's beginning to look a lot like Christmas" or "Here comes Santa Claus" with a big goofy smile on his face. I remember mom's cookies and handmade chocolates and nut rolls. The peanut butter balls that melted in your mouth and the hard tack candy that was always arriving as a gift from a neighbor. I remember Rock'em Sock'em Robots and Mattel

Electronic Football and Skittle Bowl. I have visions of Christmas dinner with Pap and great uncle Harold and cousin Virginia. The people who came to dinner and received a gift of clothing of some sort. As a kid I thought how boring it must be to not get a toy to play with. I recall with pleasure the homemade noodles which I stirred into the mashed potatoes and then mixed in a little home-made applesauce before consuming. I remember things like the 100 piece package of Bazooka gum I received one year.

These are all just memories from my own childhood. I also have a whole host of memories from Christmases with my own children. These are things I will never forget and reflect upon often. My wish for everyone this Christmas is to not be in such a hurry to get to the next big thing. Take the time to reflect on the little things that are important from the past and then slow down and enjoy the little moments from this season as well. Enjoy this moment before it is gone. Merry Christmas!

Maybe Next Year

For Christmas I bought Sally an exercise program. She had been complaining about not being happy with her body and that she felt out of shape. Sally loves to be active and fit and she never gives up when she faces a physical challenge. So I decided to give her a big challenge by ordering that 90 day intense workout muscle confusion program. It has all sorts of different exercises that you do each day so that your body never quite adapts. Each workout is an intense 60 to 90 minutes. I figured that would get her back on track.

I WAS STUPID!!!! I failed to examine the whole scenario, the whole picture. Sally has been doing this exercise program for about a week now and she is doing great. The problem is that she is making me do it with her! Yes my muscles are confused. They are wondering why in the world I am torturing them like this! It even hurts to breathe. I have needed to go downstairs for three days now but I am avoiding the trip for fear of the pain. Sitting, standing, rolling over in bed, these are all adventures in misery right now. But the worst thing is that I cannot let Sally know. I have to make her think that this is a piece of cake and of no benefit to me and my magnificently conditioned body. Maybe then she will stop making me join her for this nightly torture.

And by the way, next year for Christmas Sally is getting a massage chair and a gift card to Dairy Queen.

Every Single Day

As I get older I tend to look at the world around me with more appreciation. I tend to notice the little things again. I tend to take time to study the minor details. I take notice of the beauty in little moments. I begin to ponder my own mortality as the birthdays just keep piling up! Do you have that problem too? Are you having yet another birthday? Do the candles on your cake strike fear in the hearts of critters in the forest 5 miles away?

I have learned that instead of fearing this aging process, I tend to look at it now as an adventure. Each new year brings out some new and exciting challenge for me to face. When I was young, I had to face the challenge of shaving. Now, I have to face the challenge of shaving ear hair. Many years ago I had to learn how to comb my hair. Now I must learn how to distribute my hair evenly. In earlier times I would pull a muscle and it would be better the next day. Now it takes me until the next day to get back up when I fall down.

Every year some new body part decides to break down or not function correctly. Most of these changes are not going to kill me, but they sure make life more of a challenge. Needing to find my reading glasses just to read the instructions that came with that new gadget the kids bought is more frustrating than just figuring it out on my own. I am a man! I don't need instructions anyhow!

So, if you are having a birthday anytime soon, I hope you view it as a new chapter in this great adventure we are living. Because it truly is a blessing to be here every single day.

In the Bedroom

My bedroom is a mess. I don't understand it. I cannot ever seem to find enough places to stick all of my stuff. it is all important stuff too! Let me take inventory. On the headboard of the bed is a little wicker basket that I put stuff in at night when I go to bed. You know, stuff from my pockets. There is a bottle of vitamins, 3 books, two empty glasses (I guess I could take those to the kitchen), oops, another book, dominos (I bought those at a yard sale), a blood pressure machine (my bp is good but I like to check it sometimes), one of those things you use to scrape the dead skin off of your feet, an empty orange soda can (maybe I should throw that away) and a candle (in case the lights go out). See! All important stuff! As I look on around the room I see a 2010 calendar on the wall (well, maybe I should take that down since it is January 2011. It does have nice Norman Rockwell pictures though. Maybe I should leave it up as an "artistic piece"). Next is the top of my dresser. There is a fancy cup the kids got me for a gift, some pictures, a little statue, Christmas name tag stickers (what? I am not behind, I am just early … getting prepared for NEXT Christmas), half a package of chocolate (I'd better hide that), 2 bottles of medicine, a radio, a harmonica (never know when the urge to play a tune may hit me), my wallet and two magazines. Again, all important stuff. If I shove these things in a drawer, I will not be able to find them when I need them. As I look on around the room, I will not go into great detail, but I will give you the highlights. I see my bookcase full of books (the ones one the headboard are in case I want to read in bed and do not feel like getting up), a set of weights for exercise, the clothes I took off last night (yes I will take them to the laundry room when I head that direction), a guitar, a rocking chair, a stuffed animal the kids gave me, a fiddle my dad made, a roll of Christmas wrapping paper (what can I say, I am prepared), and a bottle of mouthwash. All important stuff. Don't you agree?

—

Last night I made some chicken and fried potatoes for dinner. I was feeling industrious and had a few leftover potatoes, so I decided to make the kids some homemade potato chips. I was not sure what their reaction would be, but as it turned out, they loved them! They were eating them faster than I could make them. It got me to thinking about how we take for granted the simple things we can do with our families and how those simple things often produce the most lasting memories. I know for me many of my best memories are of little things. I guess that in the end, the little things really are the big things because they turn out to be what matters most.

Weekend Plans

This weekend I plan to spend a lot of time watching commercials and I am excited about it. Well, let me be a bit clearer. I plan on watching some football playoff games. I recently read about a study that found that an NFL game has approximately eleven minutes of actual action. The rest of the time is spent kinda standing around. So I am gathering that in a 3 hour game, I am probably gonna watch two hours of commercials with a splash of action in between.

This study has gotten me to thinking. I bet we wouldn't see so many 300 pound linemen if they actually stopped the game clock between each play and these guys had to actually play 60 minutes of football.

Out of curiosity, I went to eBay and looked up the cost of buying tickets to the games this weekend. The going price seemed to be in the $150/ticket range. So, let's see, $150 divided by eleven minutes. That's $13 and change per minute plus gas for the car plus parking plus food per person.

I am still excited about staying home and watching the games. I can do that for free. Well, of course I will want to eat something that is bad for me, but other than that, I will have a cheap day.

Now if I can just convince Sally and the kids that it is a great day for them to go snoop around at the mall …

Tax Time

I am trying to understand taxes. Now I know that I am just an old country boy when you get right down to it, but it seems to me that there is something wrong with our system of taxation. I want to see if I can follow that path of a dollar for just a bit. I go to work and earn a dollar. Good thing! Right? Ok, so my paycheck comes and Uncle Sam takes 25 cents of that dollar. Now I have 75 cents. I take that 75 cents and go to the store to buy something. There's the dear old Governor holding out his hand for another 7%. 75 cents x 7% = 5 cents. There goes another nickel. Most likely this item I bought was imported and therefore taxed. Do you think that I am paying for that tax as part of my purchase price? You can bet your sweet bippy I am! My brief internet research found that amount to be somewhere around 17%. Well, I had 70 cents left x 17%= another 11 cents gone. My dollar has now dwindled to 59 cents. The domestic shipping costs were mainly fuel. Probably another ten cents of tax there. I could dig deeper into the effect taxes paid by the domestic supplier and delivery company and the retailer had on my purchase price and I would bet that I would get down to about a quarter of my dollar left after all of the taxes if I am lucky. But my old hillbilly brain is getting tired and I am also hungry so I am gonna go find me a snack and re-energize before I tackle any more of the world's problems today.

I have been working on getting my tax stuff together. What fun! I have a big shoebox in which I keep business receipts. All year long I have been just tossing them in there. Now I have to go through and count and add and sort them. I hate paperwork. When it comes to taxes, there are lots of decisions to make. For instance, can I deduct all of the food I ate at that festival I appeared at in October? I mean I spent a fortune on corn dogs and deep fried candy bars and funnel cakes. I think that is a business expense. Or how about this receipt for the movie theater when I took the family to see a new animated flick. With popcorn, I spent nearly $100. I can say I was doing research for my next book. Maybe I can even find a way to deduct all the money I spent at yard sales. I was merely preserving Americana. I think I am onto something here. I may get back a fortune by the time I get done!

Critical Illness

I have been ill the past several days. It all started quite innocently as what seemed like a little touch of a sinus infection last Thursday morning. It was an annoyance but little more. Over the weekend the sinus pressure was such that my eyeballs hurt. Then by Sunday evening, the body aches kicked in, I developed a low grade fever and I was freezing to death. I spent the whole day in bed Monday and the better part of Tuesday. Here it is Wednesday and I am up more but my eyeballs still ache. I am improving but too slowly for my liking. I am not sure what to call this thing I have, but I hope it goes away and stays away.

The animals have loved having me sick. They can come lay on me and I might not move for hours. Normally I do not sit still long enough at one time to make a good bed.

Also, it was not all bad for me. The timing of my illness coincided with a Star Trek marathon on television. The Insectoids and the Aquatics were at odds over whether to help or destroy the humans. I am glad they got it all worked out. It was touch and go there for a while.

I have not been able to enjoy food. I have an appetite, but everything tastes like cardboard. It takes all of the fun out of eating.

I need to go for now. There is another Star Trek episode starting. I will keep you informed.

—

The black cat at this house has got it all figured out. First of all, I must explain that my home has many windows which are basically floor to ceiling and each 4 feet wide. Cats are creatures of comfort. They plot ways to be more comfortable all of the time. The black cat here has selected a spot from which she can see out the window to watch for birds while sitting on a furnace vent with warm air blowing up her butt and still be within view of the refrigerator in case anybody decides to retrieve some turkey to share from the lunchmeat drawer. Why can't I be a cat?

Glorious Times Ahead

inally there is some sign of warmth outside! It got cold in early December and has remained cold without pause until now in mid/late February. Not that this is any heat wave, but 40s feels darned good! The weatherman says we may even hit 60 later in the week. I already went to the mailbox in my shorts yesterday. Of course I had to run back in and lock the door when all of the women from the neighborhood caught a glimpse of my sexy legs.

Through snow, sleet, freezing rain and bitter cold that mailman has never failed in his duty to deliver me bills and junk mail six days a week. He has failed miserably, however, in delivering me the money to pay for all of these things. I mean I would be happy if only one out of every one hundred pieces of mail he delivered contained money rather than a request for some of my money. Everything I get is either a request or a demand for a piece of my financial pie.

I am excited about the coming Spring. Soon there will be yard sales sprouting up all around me and I will be able to return to the Mancave to avoid all of the honey do's that Sally seems to keep creating. Glorious times are ahead! I can only imagine how good it will feel to tinker once again in peace.

Complaints

I have kept busy today. I had some work to do on the computer and I had a couple of errands to run. It has been my kind of day, busy but not hectic, working on things I enjoy. I wish every day could be like this.

For some reason many of us end up doing things we would rather not be doing for a large portion of our lives. Take yesterday, for instance, I spent over an hour on the phone arguing/debating with two different customer service agents at a company. They agreed that I had a valid point, but said that there was no one in the entire company who had the authority to fulfill my request. I am telling you that they were not being truthful. The truth is that these two people did not have the authority to fulfill my request and their job was to not let me talk to the person who did have that authority. You never get to talk to anyone who actually has the power to make a decision. According to these customer service reps, the decision makers don't even have telephones. I may look stupid, but I think they are just telling me a story. Walk through any office and every desk has a telephone. I asked them how they communicated with these decision makers and they responded that they did so by email. Yet when I asked for the email address they were unable to produce one. I think that they just wanted to get rid of me.

I also spent an extended period of time yesterday in a traffic jam. I could have had more fun if I had been at the dentist's office undergoing surgery or something. I spent an hour looking for some papers I needed. I also spent an hour in bed last night doing absolutely nothing ... too awake to sleep and too sleepy to get up. Maybe I will finish this great day with an early trip to bed to catch up on my beauty sleep. Besides, I cooked, so Sally can surely do the dishes, don't you think?

—

I made dinner this evening for the family. Homemade chicken pot pie. I must say that it came out wonderful. I have not attempted a pot pie in a very long time, but this was a hit with everyone. I made it with potatoes and carrots and pearl onions and mushrooms and peas and I also blackened the chicken ahead of time. Sally blackens most things she cooks ... eggs, toast, macaroni, broccoli, you name it, she blackens it.

Still Handsome

In general, the older I get the more I forget. I was thoroughly enjoying a scene on television of a movie the other day when Sally entered the room and said, "You already saw this. You rented it." I think she was just making stuff up, because I had never seen that movie in my life.

I sometimes fear that I will repeat myself in my writing and write a story about a subject that I have already covered. I can see it now. When I am 65, I will write a book consisting of 43 chapters, 14 of which will be about the same thing. I now understand why old men tell the same stories over and over. It is fresh and new to them each time! I guess it is God's way of keeping life interesting when you get old. I will still be trying new things, but it's nice to know that the old stuff will be new again too!

On a different note, I went to play racquetball the other day. I had not had the opportunity to do that in a while. It is one of my favorite games. It is challenging and great exercise. The next day I had a sore spot on my ankle and one on my face from where I smacked myself with the ball. Yep, for those of you who do not know racquetball, it is like tennis played in a room in which you can hit the ball off of any wall as long as it hits the front wall before it bounces. Sometimes it is best to hit the ball really hard against the back wall so that it goes all the way up and hits the front wall. However, it is best NOT to be standing there 2 feet from the back wall staring at the ball as it bounces off at a speed of like 438mph and smacks you in the face. I was quite worried that I might lose some of my handsomeness there for a minute. No need to fear. I got home and looked in the mirror and I was just as good looking as ever.

Dad and Spring

This is the first day of March. A sunny morning, a bit chilly, but to me it means Spring is here. Sure, March can have cold, snowy weather, but it is rarely long lived. But, March also can have warm, sunny days that make you get the urge to go out and plant something. I am good at finding the time to plant things. I seem to struggle more at finding time when it is time to weed things and it is 97 degrees outside.

My father always loved this time. He would have been planting onions and lettuce just any day now. He loved to get things like that from the garden. In his retired years, he spent his winters holed up in his woodshop making things and then he emerged in Spring to the outdoors to tend to his garden and the yard. It made for a good life. He was retired for 25 years before his passing. He would get up in the morning and go out to tinker for a while then come inside and sit in the recliner and play a musical instrument for a bit. He would then grab a bite to eat and then head outside to continue whatever he was working on. He was quite happy and content. I can't blame him. It sounds like a good way to go through life.

—

Sally becomes a crazy lady this time of year. She guards the thermostat like a Doberman. If she cannot see her breath, she knows that somebody has been messing with the temperature. The poor children and I run around wrapped in blankets and coats with icicles on our noses. Sally considers anything over 45 degrees in winter to be an unbearable heat wave even if it's indoors. I am in fear of freezing to death. Please help by sending firewood or old furniture for me to burn or maybe a straight jacket for me to put on Sally until spring arrives!

—

I went to some yard sales this past weekend. It is one of my favorite hobbies. I love to snoop through the various treasures being offered. The best find for me was a 4 foot long Star Trek poster that was framed. It was a cutaway of the starship Enterprise with detailed listings of where everything was located. That is pretty cool considering the ship will not even be built for like a few hundred years. Sally would say that it would look great in the garage, but I am thinking maybe more like the main living room over the fireplace! Shouldn't every home have such a masterpiece on display? Just ask any man!

Butt Sniffing

Have you ever thought about the fact that when animals meet or greet one another they always sniff? What is that all about? I was noticing the other day that even two cats in my home who are the best of buddies sniff each other every time they meet. It got me to thinking. Am I missing out on something here? Are we humans missing out on some big primal satisfaction?

I decided to give this whole sniffing thing a try with my cats. When I came into the room and they were there, I immediately ran up and sniffed them. They actually appeared annoyed by this process? Was I not doing it right? Or was there some unwritten code discouraging cross species sniffing? Next I tried it on the dog and got the same sort of reaction. I just wanted to understand. Maybe I was right about this cross species thing or perhaps it was supposed to be part of some larger ritual to which I had not fully tuned in yet.

Anyhow, I have decided that I need to try this on humans. Do you think the woman at the convenience store will mind if I ask if I can smell her before she takes my money? Maybe I can sniff the mailman too. I guess I could go to the mall and sniff people as they walk by. There has to be something to this and why should all of the other animals get to have all of the fun? You should give this a try as well. Go up to your boss at work today and take a big whiff or ask some stranger in the produce aisle at the grocery if you can smell each other. We may be starting a whole new fad here!

Stupid Neighbor

I am in the mood to go beat up my one neighbor that lives up the street. I really don't know him other than just saying hello a time or two. But today I came to the conclusion that he is not very smart and that I do not like him.

You see, he mowed his yard! Nobody else has felt the need to mow their yards yet this spring but this dummy had to go and be the first! Now my wife and the wives of all the other guys in the neighborhood will be clamoring to have their yards mowed too. They will say, "That guy up the street mowed his grass already and it is not dying." He just had to go and wimp out and ruin it for the rest of us! Winter vacation is now over thanks to him! With my luck next weekend he will probably be out there mulching or something stupid. Go inside and watch a hockey game or something on TV, dude! Don't be such a wimp!

Not Me

I quipped to a friend of mine recently that my life is like a country song. It is not entirely true because my momma has not been run over by a train yet. But, art does imitate life. And no matter how fabulous the story, it has probably happened to someone.

People just somehow get themselves into the darndest predicaments sometimes. It is often purely by accident or stupidity. I saw a video on television the other night where a guy took a Jeep up this steep hill and then got stuck halfway up. In his attempt to slowly back down he got turned sideways and ended up rolling all the way back down the hill. He was fine but the Jeep was a mess. I bet his buddies had a good laugh about that one.

Now, of course I have NEVER done anything stupid in my whole life. I was unlucky a time or two but never stupid. Well, there was that one time when I … but we won't count that. Of course maybe when Billy and I tried to fix the pool and instead ended up having to tear the whole thing down … nah, we won't count that either. I was just unlucky then. And that chicken that darned near pecked my legs off was just mean. I was just trying to play with him.

See, like I said, I have never done anything stupid! It's all those other people out there!

Shorty

There are a lot of memories that I have surrounding Easter growing up. It was usually a fairly busy time with some fun traditions. My best Easter however was the one when I had the mumps. You do not hear much about the mumps these days since they now have a vaccine for them, but I was lucky and got them right before the prevention became available. My case was not bad though. I was only minorly swollen on the sides of my neck. Nothing like some kids got.

The other reason that was a memorable Easter was because it was the same year that my dad brought Shorty home. Dad told me that Shorty's mom and dad were purebred beagles. Unfortunately, as Shorty grew, he seemed to forget this fact as he ended up growing to become a 60 pound hound dog towering far above any beagle that I had ever seen! Even with his questionable heritage, Shorty was a great dog. He was friendly and good with kids. He was always so happy to see me.

Shorty's greatest talent in life was his ability as a weatherman. He could predict thunderstorms hours in advance. He would pace back and forth all afternoon before running and hiding at the first discernable rumble. He was truly fearful of the storms.

That Easter was the beginning of a long and happy friendship between Shorty and I. He was my partner for many, many years. As Easter approaches I will make it a point to pause and recall the good times he and I had together.

—

There is a battle around my house concerning the best deviled eggs. One camp prefers the ones with mayonnaise and some other crap in them, while the intelligent side likes the ones made with mustard and vinegar and brown sugar. I will not tell you which side I am on in this battle. Truthfully, I can eat either one, but there is a big preference for the best kind. Any reasonable and sophisticated human being would come to the same conclusion while a Neanderthal might prefer the other one. I am not taking sides in this debate, even though I do actually have a preference. I would never let my bias show in my writing.

Thank You Mom

Mother's Day is a great time to appreciate mom and all that she sacrificed for you. All that she did for you out of love. My mom always gave me what she thought I needed. It was not always what I wanted, but it was almost always exactly what I needed. Like those Milk of Magnesia moments. I sure did not want that nasty tasting stuff, but I guess it worked. I am still here. I also remember her giving me those damned leftovers out of the fridge every day until they were gone. She gave me a hoe and a row of beans in the garden to work on bright and early on summer mornings and she gave me a burlap sack and a shovel when the potatoes were ready too.

Mom made sure I had clean clothes and food in my belly and respect for my elders. She made sure I knew that she would always be the boss even now when I am nearing 50 years old. She made it quite clear when she disagreed with the way I was behaving or the decisions I made and she always made sure that I understood that it was nothing personal. She did it all out of love.

So be sure to take time to thank your mom today for all that she has done for you. You may or may not have agreed with all that she did and in some cases she may not have even done her best, but remember that she is a big part of why you are here today.

I am lucky. I had a great mom and dad. My mom is 85 and quite feisty. She still makes sure that I know if I am not living up to her standards and keeps me walking the straight and narrow! She may not always make me happy with what she has to say, but she does make me a better person.

Thanks mom, for all that you have done and continue to do.

Here Jax

I was out on my bicycle today when the lady at the bank said to me, "Go home and work on your new book!"

So here I am!

What's been on my mind? Well, as always, a lot of things. But perhaps the most pressing issue for me right now is food. For instance, I am making cod for dinner tonight. I am planning to cover it in almond slices and garlic and butter. And I am making gnocchi with it just because there is nothing better than a tater dumpling. The trouble is, what do I make to go with it? I can throw some green vegetables out there and be fine, but the gnocchi needs a sauce. I was in the middle of my bike trip home when I came up with a brilliant idea … squirrel gravy! Gnocchi with squirrel gravy sounds splendid!

There is an abundance of squirrels in my suburban neighborhood, but the people here, unlike the rural areas where I grew up, tend to frown on the thought of eating them. I knew I would have a lot of angry soccer moms if I took out the shotgun and started to round me up a mess. I needed to get creative!

It was then that the inspiration hit me! I pulled my bike to the side of the street and proceeded to tie acorns to the spokes of my wheels. I then just simply rode slowly through the neighborhood. Heck, it is not my fault that the squirrels just kept running into my tires! And I was doing the neighborhood a favor by offering to take them home and "dispose of them properly" in a potful of gravy. I am quite proud of myself! I am a genius!

Now I am thinking already about tomorrow's dinner! Roasted duck perhaps? Or maybe grilled Schnauzer? I know someone who owns a Schnauzer named Jax! He looks well fed! I wonder how he would taste with mint jelly! Heeeere Jax! Here boy!

The Latest News

The lady at the bank has been complaining again that I am not writing enough and you know what? She is right. I have a lot to say and who wouldn't want to listen to my wonderful words of wisdom anyhow?

I have been pondering lots of important things recently. Although I really can't remember what any of them are at the moment. Hey! It's late! Almost midnight! I am sure they will come to me at about 4am.

I did have a funny conversation with a friend of mine who works for the service department of a high end auto dealership. We were discussing how fun it would be if we could call the customers with some interesting news. For instance, "Mrs. Johnson, could you please return your Mercedes to the dealership using all right turns? We seem to have found some extra lug nuts that may belong to you." or perhaps "Mr. Lane, one of our technicians was injured while working on your car. Would you please check the trunk for a size 9 index finger and get back to us if you find it? Its owner would really like to have it back."

I also have a friend with a houseboat on a lake. I was talking with them about how cool it would be to have a remote controlled dorsal fin to scare the crap out of their neighbors.

I bought a unicycle at a yard sale recently. I am sure I am keeping the neighbors highly entertained as I try to conquer this beast. My children are probably just embarrassed as usual at dad's latest stunt.

I had an interesting grilling experience the other night. I had hamburgers and hot dogs all coming along nicely when a gusty storm started to move into the area. The winds were upwards of 50 miles per hour as I was trying to chase hot dogs flying through the air. It was an adventure to get dinner to the table.

As I write this my cat has decided to eat my strawberry yogurt. I would never dream that he would steal that. Of course one of the cats like marshmallows, so I guess that is stranger.

Elizabeth graduated high school and will be headed to college in the fall. Shelly got her own apartment and then got mad at me because I was still trying to be dad. Will just keeps smiling every day. He is the happiest kid I know. He is supposed to be studying for his driver test but he just keeps playing video games and hanging out. I guess he is not ready to grow up yet and that is ok by me. I am not ready to grow up yet either.

Today is a significant day of sorts for me. 1 year ago today I had a mild stroke. It was a very scary event filled with a lot of uncertainty which made this past year even more eventful with tests and procedures and such. But here I am one year later still kicking! That is a big positive for me! I treasure every day and every moment and every person a little more.

Well, there you have it! You are all caught up on the news! I will try to be more diligent so that lady at the bank will stop bugging me. Actually, I like the fact that she works to keep me on track. It is good for me.

Happy 94

Today would have been my dad's 94th birthday. He has been gone over 5-and-one-half years now. Yes, I still miss him and yes, it will always be that way. He was a great man. He was a common man, but a great man. He was the man who always tried to do the right thing. I did not always agree with him or always think he was doing what was best, but I always knew that his intentions were to do it right. And truthfully he succeeded at doing the right thing 99.9% of the time. What more could you ever ask for.?

I wish I could be a fraction of the man he was. I never doubted his integrity or his honesty even when it was not what I wanted to hear. He worked hard all of his life. And he played clean. He loved music and children and gardens and woodworking and cooking and dogs. Dad was not much of a socialite. He became quite anxious in public making the whole ordeal uncomfortable for him yet he frequently tolerated his anxiety to be a part of the world around him. He was most at ease just kicked back in his recliner with a musical instrument in hand playing and singing a happy tune.

I learned a lot from the man. The greatest lessons he taught me become ever more apparent as my own life grows and matures. His example of how to live is one I hope I can grow into someday.

Regional Foods

Foods that you can find in various regions around the country can be so vastly different. I have lived in a few different states and visited many others and it is always a great experience to sample the local cuisine. Here in Indiana, for instance, they seem to have a running competition for the best fried pork tenderloin sandwich. The meat is cut thin and heavily breaded. They are almost always 3 times the size of the bun. In Tennessee the 3 things you saw everywhere were sweet tea, catfish and barbeque. Their barbeque was more of a smoked meat with a thin, runny sauce added later. Barbeque itself is so different from region to region. Of course those crazy Californians have a cuisine all their own with fish tacos and vegetable wraps etc. ... And there is that place for hot dogs there ... I think its called Pinks. They do some strange stuff with a hot dog.

Even hot dogs vary from town to town. The chili sauce is different. The dogs are different colors. Some places love ketchup (or catsup depending on where you are from), some hot dog joints do not allow you to get ketchup on their dog. In Florida I tested the local swamp cabbage and cheese balls made with alligator. In

Pennsylvania, my dad used to go out and find his own greens in spring. Where I live now they are out to kill all the dandelions. My dad was out to eat them. I grew up eating French fries with gravy on them. People in other parts of the country think that is pure insanity. And speaking of Crazy Californians, I once told one of them I liked peanut butter and pickle sandwiches and the first thing they did was ask me if I was pregnant. I guess they don't know what high class cuisine is like out there.

My Medical Assistant

It has been one of those kinds of weeks. I have a pinched nerve of some sort causing nerve pain on the one side of my rib cage. It is a big time nuisance because my shirt rubbing against it is uncomfortable. So I stopped in to see the doctor and what does he do? He rammed a needle right into that same area of my ribs, not once, not twice, no not three times! He gave me six injections in there. I felt like a human dart board.

All of these things that seem to go wrong with my body along the way makes me wonder if I should get my own personal Medical Assistant. Maybe a cute one with blonde hair or maybe even pink. Just so she is not a mean blue haired old lady. I deserve a pretty one, the kind old men flirt with and other women hate. Don't you think?

She could handle my appointments and my at home treatments, things like back rubs and earwax cleanings and back hair braiding and cooking dinner and mowing the lawn … What? Well, just because she is in medicine doesn't mean she doesn't know how to cut grass, right? She can take care of those kinds of things while I take my nap. Then when I wake up I will be ready for my sponge bath and pedicure.

This whole notion sounds very reasonable to me!

Food Fetish

I have been keeping an eye on the foods I eat in recent months even more than usual. I am typically a healthier eater than most but recently I have been redoubling my efforts. It is not always easy, but I am trying to stay the course. Every now and then I do like a treat. Some of my treats are healthy and some of them are not. The key is moderation.

Sometimes I feel I am just a big overgrown kid. For example, I love chocolate milk. I just do. I could drink 7 glasses a day if I could get away with it. I battle this urge by treating myself to a small glass at bedtime some nights. I also have found that I can substitute the soy milk products which come in chocolate and be satisfied as well.

Another weakness of mine is ice cream. I simply love the stuff. I like chocolate, or peanut butter … a peanut butter milkshake is like heaven in a cup. That moosetracks ice cream is quite awesome in its own right. I like just about any flavor actually, except for that mint crap. Who is the dummy who decided to spoil perfectly good ice cream by throwing some mint in there.

"Oh honey, your breath smells so fresh!"

"Why thank you! I just polished off a gallon of mint rocky road!"

Disgusting I tell you! Plain disgusting!

I have many other weaknesses like cooked pudding (so much better than the instant stuff). I like rice and tapioca the best. Jell-O. Pumpkin Pie. No Bake Cookies. I could go on and make a massive list but these are just a few of my favorites.

I even had a big bowl of Lucky Charms the other night and you know what? They really still are magically delicious. Remember anything is ok in moderation. Those little marshmallows in Lucky Charms are pretty cool.

Speaking of marshmallows, those are another weakness of mine that I have rediscovered quite recently. I just have the urge to eat a whole big bag or two. Of course, on the good side of things, I have also been craving Navel Oranges lately. Not sure why, but they have been on my mind a lot. Maybe I could make a delicious and satisfying midnight feast by combining the two. I think it might go quite good together! Navels and marshmallows! What do you think? I think I am ready to try some right now!

My Drug Problem

My insurance recently switched to mail order for prescriptions. I am not happy about it! I like to deal with the local pharmacist who I know and trust. This is just another computer I have to talk to at another impersonal company. And just to prove its silliness, let me tell you about the two prescriptions I have received recently.

The first was for a little pill I can take as needed. Its prescription reads that I may take from one-half to two pills every four hours as needed. For me that is something I take about 1/2 a pill a month. The mail order pharmacy filled my prescription by sending me one thousand four hundred forty of these little pills. At the rate I am currently using them, I have enough to last me until about the year 2250 at which time I will be 288 years old. No, this is not an exaggeration. Actually the year 2251 would be more accurate.

The other prescription which I received today after running out of it last week because it was lost in the mail somewhere … good thing it was not like heart medicine or something … is prescribed for me to take one to three per day. I typically use one. I received 300 of those at a total cost to me of $60 and a total cost to the insurance company of $2305.78. Also in today's mail was a letter from my insurance company informing me that effective the first of the month, that particular medicine that I just happened to receive today is no longer going to be covered under my particular insurance plan. Wow! What a coincidence! The letter did state, however, that shotgun shells to put me out of my misery would be covered at full cost (limit 3 per customer).

Missing Shelly

Kids! They are the source of some of the greatest blessings and greatest heartbreaks in life. I have been blessed with three wonderful children of my own and 4 special stepchildren. Each one brings something unique to my life.

I have been very lucky. My kids have managed to avoid trouble and have grown into wonderful young adults with huge potential ahead of them. I will never stop being a dad, but my raising job is nearly complete.

It's that never stop being a dad thing that seems to have gotten me on my oldest daughter Shelly's bad side. She got mad at me on Easter and has rarely spoken to me since except to yell at me. I did not agree with how she was handling something so I spoke my mind and gave her a father/daughter lecture. Shelly is twenty and I know at that age I felt I knew everything I needed to know too. It is a common ailment. I recently was talking to a nephew who is in his early thirties and he simply nodded knowingly as he recalled those days with a smile.

"We all go through that stage!" he said.

It is so true. The older I get, the dumber I realize I am.

As a parent, I know I will not always say what my children want to hear nor will I always be right, but I will still always say what I feel I need to say because I love them and have their best interests at heart.

My mom is the same way. The last time I was home she told me I needed to color my hair because I was looking old! How dare her! Me? Old? Hair color? She simply spoke what was on her mind whether I liked it or not. That is part of what I love about her. She gives it to me straight even when it hurts.

As for Shelly, she is a great young woman with a lot of talent, a good heart and huge potential in life. I hope that she will come to realize that dad was just being dad and that no matter what she does it will never change the fact that I love her. She can be mad at me and yell at me now and then , but I will still want her to come by and play Frisbee with the old man just like we always have.

Gas, Nuts and Bottles

I went to the grocery store today to pick up a few items I needed for dinner. As I was driving home mourning the loss of such a large sum of cash, I noticed the price at the gas station I was passing. It is a sad day when I was happy to see that gas was now down to $3.45 a gallon for regular unleaded. The sign also listed diesel at $3.99, Mid Grade at $3.55 and Premium at $3.65. Of course, as usual, this got me to thinking.

First of all, I realized that many people around today do not realize that when I was young what they call regular today was just called unleaded. And regular was leaded gasoline. I really don't know if it was a pollution issue or an economic issue or what the problem was with leaded gas but they stopped selling it at some point in the 1970's. It was what most people used since it was the cheapest.

Next I got to thinking about the three grades of gas available today. Diesel was not part of this question since it is a totally different animal and if you accidentally put diesel in a non-diesel engine, bad things tend to happen. I am no mechanic, but I heard that on "Car Talk" so it has to be true. Anyhow, I was pondering the gasoline available. First of all, the regular unleaded works just fine for most cars and is the cheapest, so therefore I would assume by far the most popular kind of gas. There are then some high performance cars in which they tell you to only use the premium stuff which works better in those engines. None of my cars has ever been a high performer, but I do sometimes give them a tank of the good stuff if they are running funny. I am not sure if it helps, but it makes me feel like I am doing something. Finally, there is the Mid-Grade. What the heck is the purpose of that stuff? I do not know that I have ever pulled up to a pump and decided that I needed a tank full of Mid-Grade gas. And come to think of it, I don't recall ever having heard anyone ask for Mid-Grade in a gas station. In my mind either you want the good stuff or the cheap stuff, not the semi-good middle of the road stuff. They can't be selling much of it. So why even keep it around?

Of course I guess I am just not enlightened enough to the ways of the world. I have never bought small eggs at the store either. I bought mediums if they were on sale maybe, but mostly I just wanted the large ones. Why are they sold in different sizes? I mean, I realize that chickens don't all lay the same size eggs, but I would think that the off sizes would be used in other products rather than sold at the store. Maybe I just have too much time on my hands to think these days. Maybe people will think I am nuts for worrying about gas and eggs.

Speaking of nuts, who decides what mixture of nuts to put in a can of mixed nuts because I would like to have a word with them too. They always either have too many peanuts in them or if I buy the "premium mixture to get away from the peanuts then they put those disgusting Brazil nuts in there. Don't get me wrong. I like peanuts just fine. But when I want peanuts I will get a jar of peanuts. A can of mixed nuts should not consist of 17

Brazil nuts, 2 Cashews, and 3 Filberts. I want a can equally full of Cashews, Pecans, Macadamias, Filberts and Almonds. Now that would be a can of nuts worth buying. I hope Mr. Planters is reading this right now.

Actually if the world would listen to me, I have lots of great ideas. I want my pop in glass bottles. By the way , did you know that where I grew up in Pennsylvania, if I wanted a Mountain Dew I would say I wanted a pop and then they would say what kind and I would say Mountain Dew. In other places I have been you would ask for a soda and go though the same process. And when I lived in Tennessee I would say I want a coke and they would say what kind of coke do you want and then I would say Mountain Dew. If I asked for a pop there they would just look at me funny.

And finally there is this pancake issue. I love pancakes. Actually my favorites are Buckwheat cakes with real maple syrup and a hint of butter. To me there is nothing better. But around here where I live now, the first thing they do when you slap a pancake down in front of them is cover it in peanut butter! What a waste of good peanut butter and a good pancake. I mean I thought everybody knew that peanut butter went best on a sandwich with pickles!

Air Conditioned Heaven

This has been one of the most stiflingly hot days I have ever experienced. I don't fully understand why. I have endured temperatures over 100 for the better part of a month in Tennessee in the past and lots of humidity, but today here in Indiana I had sweat pouring from every pore in my body. The humidity had to be very high. I never knew my eyeballs could sweat like that.

I have been hiding in the air-conditioning here at home tonight. The AC unit is working very hard to keep me comfy. When I was a kid in Pennsylvania, nobody had air conditioning. It was a luxury to go into a store in town that had some. I guess we were ok because we were not spoiled by it. I do know that we had certain processes to keep things as cool as possible. The first thing you did in the morning was close all windows and blinds. This was to keep the cooler night air in and the warmer day air out. Then as it began to get a little stuffy along about 10 or 11am, you would turn the fan on low. Most houses only had one fan. By about 3 in the afternoon all of the coolness was gone. You then simply opened the windows and turned the fan on high and laid in front of it.

When evening came, all activities transferred to the outdoors. This is why older homes have big front porches because people actually used them every day. It was where life took place until , and sometimes well after, dark. People would typically turn the fan to blow the hot air out during the evening and then turn it around to blow cool air in at bedtime. This process was then repeated the next morning. I bet you never knew there was a science to keeping cool, did you?

I have also read somewhere that air-conditioning has contributed to obesity. Keeping your own body cool apparently burns calories. When we live in an air-conditioned world we just get fatter. Well, I can certainly say that I am fatter now than when I did not have air conditioning. And to think I was trying to blame that problem on ice cream.

Speaking of which, there was nothing better on a hot summer evening than a bowl of ice cream. My mom did not believe in just having the plain old flavors of chocolate, vanilla and strawberry either. We had fudge ripple and raspberry and maple walnut and butterscotch and even various flavors of sherbet. No we did not have them all at once. She just rotated and you got the one she had or nothing at all. It was your choice.

So tonight I think I am gonna turn off the A/C and burn off enough calories to have me a big bowl of Maple Walnut ... on second thought, I have already sweat enough today. I think I will eat the ice cream and leave the A/C alone.

Cat Talk

The old cat is giving me trouble. You see, I went to the store the other day and bought some good turkey breast and she knows it. She has been stalking me. Every time my foot lands on the kitchen floor she is there. "Meow! Meow! Meow!" which translates, "Give me the turkey fool!"

I don't know how she does it. I can check and find her sleeping clear across the house and tiptoe all the way to the kitchen and there she is, "Meow! Meow! Meow!" I think she may have installed a surveillance system or something. Or maybe she has Fuzzbutt and the others on sentry duty for her.

And don't you dare try and con her with the cheap stuff. She will have no part of it. The big problem is gonna come in a couple of days when the turkey is all gone. No matter how much I try to explain it to her, she never believes me. She just sits there, "Meow! (Liar!) Meow Meow! (Damned Liar get me some turkey!)." And so I usually end up giving in and making a trip to the store.

Cravings

I have been craving pork rinds. It's true! I love the darned things and recently I have had the strong urge to eat a bunch of them. My favorites used to come from a flea market in Bowling Green, Kentucky. There were some people who made them right there on the spot and then seasoned them with all sorts of different things. I always liked the plain, old fashioned ones, but the ranch ones were darned good as well. They are a great snack for everybody at my house. Even the dogs and cats think this is great stuff.

I seem to bounce from one craving to the next. Recently it was marshmallows. Can't get enough of them. And I also have been on a root beer kick. Cantaloupe! I could eat a whole one myself. Corn on the cob. I grill it in the husk and then eat 7 or 8 ears in a sitting.

I wonder where cravings come from. They are ever changing. Does anybody out there crave the same things as me? Is there somebody sitting in St. Louis right now thinking, "Boy I wish I had some pork rinds!" or anybody in Alaska saying, " What have I gotta do to get a good juicy cantaloupe?"

I even crave water on a hot summer day. Good cold water! I can drink a gallon of anything else and I still want water. Some people say your body craves what it needs. So maybe I am needing pork rinds! That's it! I need to eat them for my health! Come to think of it I am craving ice cream too ... and sausage gravy and biscuits ... and ...

Air Conditioner Repair

I was in a parking lot earlier today talking with an older woman I know. She walks with a cane and has a service dog and generally seems to have many health issues. She asked me a very unusual question.

She said, "Do you know which thing it is you hit to make the Air Conditioning work?"

I looked at her a bit baffled for a moment before telling her that no I did not know how to fix an Air Conditioner.

She then said, "It's a pink thing in the engine! (you big dummy) You hit it and the air comes back on."

I was absolutely clueless and I am sure it showed. She then asked me to follow her to her car. She popped open the hood and had me to lift it up and secure it for her. She then pointed to an electrical connector with a red rubber housing over it on the side of the engine.

"That's it!" she proclaimed, "That's the thing you hit!"

I looked at her doubtfully. She then went around and started her car and then returned to the front. Next, she lifted her wooden cane and began whacking that electrical connector. I truly thought she was nuts by this time. After eight or ten hits, she went back around and got into her car.

She stuck her head out the window and said," I told you! (you big dummy) It's all fixed now!"

Needless to say I will never forget the day an old woman fixed an Air Conditioner with a cane.

Nostalgic Music

I was in a music/movie store today. They had the usual selection of CDs, DVDs, BluRays and the like. However, I was
shocked and surprised at the selection of NEW record albums.
Yes, vinyl 33 rpm records! They actually had a big display of
them with music both old and new. Anything from Queen to the
soundtrack from Twilight. Is there really that good of a market
out there? I can understand the "old school" enthusiasts who
would buy old records, but who is the market for the new ones?
These albums were anywhere from $19.95 to $24.95 each, so
they were not cheap. It was kinda cool for me to see this throw-
back to my youth.

It got me to thinking that maybe the 8 track player will make
a comeback too! I would give anything to have my old bright
blue Realistic 8 track boom box. That thing was awesome! It
sounded great and was able to go anywhere I went. And talk
about durable! That thing was even dropped out of a school
bus window onto the pavement and still worked like a champ!
Let's see you try that with an iPod. I need to look on Ebay for
my old 8 track player. I would love to own one today just like

it. That is my only hope since Radio Shack barely carries radios anymore. I used to love going in that store and snooping around at all the gadgets. Now they are basically a cell phone store and that makes old guys like me quite sad.

I Need More Fun

What do you do for fun? What provides you entertainment and enjoyment? How often do you do these things? How often do you make time for fun in your life?

I ask these questions because I am realizing that I am somehow missing the fun train too often these days. There are some things I enjoy doing that I have not done in a long, long time. For instance, I love to play golf. And I am not some Johnny come lately to this. I was playing golf back in the 1970s as a teen when it was very uncool to play golf. I just enjoy the game. Curt and I used to play on a course that was lighted for night play on Friday nights. A full sized lighted course is just unheard of, but we lived near one. I am surprised that with golf's popularity today that there are not more lighted courses. It was a great way to enjoy the sport, except when you hooked one into the woods. We did lose more balls but it was worth it.

I love to play Frisbee. Sounds simple enough. Yet I have not played all summer. I used to always play with Shelly, but she has not been around this summer. It sucks when your kids grow up and move away. They have been my excuse to act like a kid myself and now they are getting into their own lives.

I have not been on my bicycle nearly enough or played basketball or racquetball in a long time. I haven't been playing my
drums or Bocce Ball. I haven't even had time for tinkering in the
Mancave.

Work, work, work. Pay bills, fix stuff, chores. What the heck
kind of fun is that? Can't I just be 10 years old again? Plus I do all
of this work and then Congress can't decide on how to properly
handle the debt problem because they are too preoccupied with
getting re-elected so my money I am saving for retirement starts
disappearing. I lost a few thousand dollars last week and I worked
hard. Who took my money? I am thinking it was Jennifer Lopez.
I just read that she signed on to be a judge for 1 more year at
American Idol for $20 million. I am gonna call American Idol
and tell them I will do the exact same job as her for $1 million.
I will only stay for 1 year and then I will retire. Then they can
pass the job on to somebody else. Look at all the money they will
save by hiring me. I promise to work very hard and do my best
for them. I will even sweep up the studio after the show. I bet
Jennifer doesn't do that.

Or maybe I need to call that lady at the bank. It is her bank
that had my money and now it is gone. I am curious who she gave
it to. I am betting it was not given to some poor person in a third
world country because they wouldn't qualify. It is more likely she
gave my money to somebody like Jennifer who already has way
too much of it to start with.

That is what I will do. When the mortgage company calls
this month demanding their money, I am telling them to call
Jennifer.

My Latest Inventions

I have been wondering about inventions again. We all just kind of accept many of the things we have as the best way to do things. I believe I may be the next Thomas Edison if I just put my mind to it. Here are some of the projects I think I should be working on.

The toilet. Is this the absolute best way we can come up with for handling human waste? The thing is awkward and clunky and clogs up all the time. I think something that incorporates a water hose and one of those high energy blow dryers like they have in the bathroom at the mall would be much more efficient. Now I know that bidets are popular in some places but I am thinking I can come up with a better solution.

Carpet. Have you ever looked closely at the underside of a piece of carpet that has been on the floor a while? It is disgusting! There are bound to be things growing under there. I am not sure what we can use instead but there has to be an alternative that is still squishy to the toes.

Campfire Sticks. I am not sure what the proper term for them is, but how many hot dogs and marshmallows have met an untimely death from a lack of a good design.

Light Bulbs. The problem here is that there are like 14,000 different kinds these days. Why? Why is it necessary to have so many different shapes and sizes and bases?

Cell Phones. It will be my goal to make a cell phone that lasts longer than the service contract.

Socks. I intend to make the world a better place by establishing an orphaned sock website.

Dishwasher. Why have one when every woman thinks you still need to rinse the dishes before you put them in there. I am making one with a built-in garbage disposal.

Politician. I want to develop one who can think for himself outside of party lines.

These are just a few of my ideas. I will continue to work on them for the benefit of all mankind.

School Supplies

Yesterday was the first day of school here. Somehow I got elected to go out this evening and collect school supplies from the lists I was given. First of all, where I came from there were no such things as school supply lists. Everything you needed was simply given to you at school. Paper, pencils, erasers, etc.. Everything was supplied for the education which we were all "entitled" to receive.

The state where I live now is even in the business of "renting" textbooks. At the price they charge for rent, I would hate to see what they would charge to buy the darned thing. There is no reason for ANY book to cost that much. Somebody is getting rich in this deal, I am afraid.

In addition to the few hundred dollars in book rent, they sent home these lists of supplies they needed in order to educate my child. Paper, pencils, folders, tabs for folders, highlighters, permanent markers, pens, scientific calculators, hole punches, index cards, Kleenex, pencil holding bag, flash drive and 379 other miscellaneous items. That big school must be empty!

So, upon being administered smelling salts, I resigned myself to the fact that I was stuck with this chore. But I was the man with the plan. While everyone else rushed off to the big department stores for this junk, I was going to sneak by the out of the way office supply store that never seems to have more than two customers in it at a time … except for tonight when there were 512 frantic mothers and their children rushing about my quiet little hidden office supply store just grabbing everything in sight!

I ventured inside figuring it was too late to turn back now. There were no carts or baskets up front, so I found a weak looking ten-year-old in the back aisle and tackled her at the knees. I then scurried away with HER cart as she ran away crying and looking for her mommy to tell on me. Who are people gonna believe? Me? Or some whining ten-year-old?

I started down the list and was getting quite frustrated. Many of the items I was searching for were out of stock except for the ones I was seeing in other peoples carts! I quickly devised a new plan to outsmart the system. A pack of pencils out of this cart and a three ring binder out of that one … I wasn't stealing and they would never miss these things until they got home! Right?

I had found my own ingenious way to express shop in a crowd. I was just about finished. I only needed a pencil sharpener. But nobody seemed to have one. I searched shelves and carts and a few children … nothing. Just then I spotted it. The lone last pencil sharpener in the whole store hanging from a lowly hook in a half hidden location. I was 10 feet and three thirtysomething year old women away from glory! I noticed one of them eyeing that same green two holed beauty. I guess they thought I would play fair since they were girls. I got my sharpener and I hear they are all recovering just fine up at community hospital.

My last hurdle was the checkout line. Every lane was 30 deep. I selected one and conveniently developed the nastiest most contagious sounding cough you have ever heard. Amazingly my line cleared one by one with amazing speed. So now another few hundred dollars later my kids are ready for another year of public education. No wonder so many kids go to private schools these days. It's probably cheaper!

Capades

I have been pondering some of the words I hear on a regular basis and while I know what they are talking about I have no idea what the words mean. Have I lost you yet? Ok, pop quiz! Put down your mouse! Hands off the keyboard! No Googling! Give me the definition for the word "capade". And you cannot use the word "ice"! C'mon, what are you waiting for? Ok, time's up! The definition of "capade " is ... actually after doing a little research I found that capade is not considered to be a real word. Kinda like "ain't". I was amazed. I even went to dictionary.com and there was nothing. So then my question is, what the heck is an "Ice Capade"? I would have assumed it meant show or extravaganza or something.

There, haven't I amazed you today?

The Old Folks Home

I stopped at a local department store the other day to pick up a package of new underwear and a bottle of baby aspirin and bananas. Not sure why I feel so worked up about bananas these days. Oh what an exciting life I am leading! So I made my purchase and on my way out I spotted an instant lottery ticket machine. Being the wild and crazy, livin' on the edge kind of guy that I am, I whipped out a five dollar bill and slid it into the bill acceptor. I made my selection of a ticket offering a top prize of $125,000! I was ready to win big! I pulled a nickel out of my pocket and began to scratch away. I was holding my breath knowing my life was about to change! I was prepared to let out a big whooping yell when I won all that money! And guess what? I won! I was so incredibly proud of myself. I had pushed the right button on the right machine at the right moment and I had won! I had beaten the odds! My life was exciting! I went up to the customer service counter to claim my $15 prize ... Oh wait ... did you think I had won the grand prize? Well no not exactly but I was still living the good life on my $10 windfall. I was thinkin' I might even use it to try out a stack of harvest nut and grain pancakes over at that new IHOP that just opened up. Talk about a party!

So now I was all proud and pumped as I exited the store with my winnings in hand. Right outside the door was a mini bus from the Sunny Horizons Retirement Community according to the sign on its side. It was loading up a bunch of blue haired ladies to take them back home. They were probably heading back for the afternoon bingo games or something. It was then that I noticed the rest of the writing on the side of the bus. It said "Rental property living for adults 55 and over". Hey wait a minute! 55? I will be 49 before too much longer so you mean to tell me I am only six years from qualifying for a retirement home! Not me! I am young and vibrant and I lead an exciting life! I mean, just that day alone I was at the store buying aspirin and ... underwear ... and ... oh crap!

Well I guess there is one good thing about all of this. I can't wait to call my brother Charles and tell him that he is ALREADY old enough to be shipped off to that place!

My Body's Secret Life

I have a splotch of paint on my big toe. I have a streak of white silicone caulk on the butt of my pants. I have a scratch on the top of each of my feet and one on my shin. I have a red sore spot on my forearm. I have a big purple bruise on my left ankle.

If I were to do a full inspection, I am sure I would find many more things wrong with my body.

These are just the ones I can spot without a mirror. What makes these things even more interesting to me is that even though I constantly live inside the body, I honestly have no idea how any of these thing occurred.

Yes, I was painting the hall yesterday evening, but I had on shoes and socks. So how did my big toe end up with paint on it? The caulk? I replaced a broken window pane and I caulked the edges. But I swear I was facing the window the whole time. My butt was never involved in the process. The scratches? One runs up and down and the other side to side. They look like they should have been painful, but I never felt a thing. The red spot on my arm would appear to be a mild burn though that is only a guess. The bruise on my ankle is a good inch and a half in diameter and purple like someone smacked me with a metal pipe. That had to hurt!

This is all a big mystery to me. It makes me wonder what else my body may be doing when I am not watching.

Growth Spurt

I feel like a kid inside and now I have proof that I am still growing. Yes, it is true that like many people my age, I am fighting my body's urge to grow outward in the wrong directions. But this is different. I have solid proof that I have not even fully blossomed yet, let alone hit my prime! The best is yet to come!

So, you ask, how do I know this? It's my feet. Yes my feet. You see, I went to buy a new pair of sneakers the other day ... and why are they called sneakers anyway? That's a whole nuther day of research for me. Anyhow, I went to the store to buy shoes that make uncoordinated people feel athletic ... there ... how's that? So I found me a nice pair that made me look all cool and stuff, but when I tried them on, they did not fit!

Let me digress a bit. When I was 18, I wore a size 10. By age 30, I was up to a 10 1/2. By age 40, I was buying mostly 11's. But the other day an 11 was too short and all tight. I have now graduated to a 12! I am still growing!

Now there was this one comment from a so-called friend with whom I shared this news, that my butt was getting so big that my feet were having to spread out to support it, but we won't pay any attention to this poor, misinformed fool.

Everybody else realized that I am truly still a kid … a bouncing baby boy … still wet behind the ears … what does that mean anyhow?

So anyway, I will be walking around and running and jumping and pretending to be a superhero in my new size 12's today. So if you see me, be sure to compliment me on how good I look and on how sharp my new shoes look on me. Maybe I should go shopping for a cape to ensemblize the outfit! I wonder where Batman and superman buy theirs?

Remodel and Repair

I have been on a fix the house kick recently. I painted the hallway and replaced the side panel window by the front door. I hung new light fixtures in the stairway to the basement and the front entryway. Today Will helped me pull out some old hedge bushes in front on the house. I would hook a chain to them and Will would pop the clutch on the tractor and take off yanking the bush out by its roots and dragging it down to the woods. He thought that was the coolest job ever!

I have just been having fun tinkering. I seem to go through stages with this. If I can keep this up for six months, I may actually run out of things to do! I want to put in some new flooring and a stone backsplash and fix that place in the sidewalk out front. I have this big long list.

I enjoy doing the work myself and saving money. This does not mean things always go smoothly. While painting the hallway, I spilled paint three different times and had to spend even more time cleaning up my mess. When I fixed the window, I must have missed a sliver of glass in my cleanup. Will found it with his foot a few days later. The light fixture hanging went well but it is a wonder I did not fall off that ladder precariously hanging over the stairwell.

The worst thing for me about this type of work is finding the tools. I tear up the Mancave looking for the stuff I need and then while doing the job I will relose, hunt for, and refind the same tools five times or more. For me, cleaning up my messes and hunting for my stuff takes way longer than the actual job. I do not want to hire someone to do the work, but maybe I should consider hiring someone to do the tool finding and mess cleanup. Also, they could be on standby to finish the job in case I get bored with it.

Anyhow, enough rambling for tonight. I have worked hard today. I deserve some ice cream.

Leaf Blower

I was talking to a friend the other day about the recent fall weather we have been experiencing. One week ago it was 100 degrees, today it is 63 and overcast with a breeze. It feels quite pleasant. We got to talking about how the leaves will soon begin to change and fall. I love that time of year. My friend, however, was lamenting the upcoming issue of raking. "I hate to rake all of those leaves!" I suggested letting the wind take care of it and just blow them all over to the neighbor's yard. This plan was shot down due to the lack of control of the direction of the wind. I was not about to be defeated in this argument. From this discussion was born a new business venture.

I am planning to run down to the local home improvement store and pick up a half dozen of those great big five foot tall fans. For a fee, I will place them in your yard in the evening. You can simply turn them on at bedtime and by morning your troubles will be all gone! Then I will come along and retrieve my fans and place a business card in your neighbor's mailbox and repeat the process by blowing those leaves on down the street. It is the fool who refuses to pay who will get stuck with the raking job and I will get rich!

Pork Festival

Today I am going to a Pork Festival. I love festivals. They are a lot of fun to me. They are my chance to eat all of the foods I am not supposed to eat. Sure there will be crafts and games and rides, but I am there for the funnel cakes and deep fried Snickers and alligator on a stick.

This particular festival has a tent that stretches what must be a city block where you can get a pork chop as big as your head along with all the fixins. And then right next door is a ladies auxiliary offering strawberry shortcake sundaes. Of course I cannot pass up the homemade footlong corn dogs or that place that has the big ears of corn on the cob. Then there is the grilled teriyaki chicken place and the one where you can have your choice of cotton candy or big pretzels with toppings. That place down on the corner is run by a fraternal lodge and serves pulled pork barbeque, but I wont go there because the one man working there was very rude to me one year. Otherwise, I am looking forward to tasting that blueberry flavored popcorn that one lady makes and maybe just a bite of the frozen chocolate covered bananas at the trailer up by the rides.

Where else but a festival can you find such a buffet? So if I do not eat myself to death I will be back here tomorrow to tell you about my experience. And if I die with an elephant ear hanging out of my mouth just know that I went a happy man.

Forward one day … I survived the festival, although it was touch and go there for awhile. I spent most of my day today with a deep fried hangover. It was worth it … for me at least. I am not speaking for that poor unfortunate soul who tried to steal a fried pickle from my plate. I sampled the flavored popcorns and the pork chops and tater salad and cole slaw and a strawberry shakeup and pork rinds, just to name a few. There were lots of people there. The weather was good. Then the plague came.

I had been at the festival for about an hour enjoying the sights and sounds when suddenly, without reason, the bugs came. Some kind of yellowish nonstinging flying bug similar to a firefly. I am not talking a few. They suddenly appeared by the thousands like a giant swarm, landing on arms and legs and ice cream cones … oh yeah, I had one those too … and in women's hair. The place suddenly changed from a festival to some sort of freakish dance contest. Just land a couple of those bugs on a 50 year old woman and you may see moves never seen before. It was horrible. They were everywhere. The bugs and the dancing women both. I was afraid to get anything else to eat because I did not want to share it with the bugs. So I decided to leave the festival early. Then something really strange happened. As soon as you exited the festival grounds, the bugs were gone. Apparently they had come for the food too! Who knew bugs had a weakness for lemon shakeups and elephant ears?

Fatherly Pride

I am so proud of my children. I know that many parents feel like that, but I can only speak for myself. In spite of all of the mistakes I may have made along the way, my kids have turned out ok. We have our ups and downs. Heck Shelley has been mad as a hornet at me about something that happened several months ago. But it doesn't mean I am any less proud of her. I still know that she is being a good citizen in this world. And Will knows that I have no idea what he is talking about when he gets all excited about something in a video game he played. He will still tell me the whole story even though he could tell me the same thing in Latin and I would understand about the same amount. He just wants me to know. All I need to know is that he is always smiling and happy 99% of the time. He is another good person. Elizabeth is off at college for her first year. She is after me constantly to make sure I did this or that for her. But she also is a caring soul inside. She has even chosen a major that will lead to a career in helping people.

All of my kids have their moments when I could just kick them in the butt, but in the final analysis, I think they are turning out to be the kind of people I hoped they would be. None of them are just like me, but they all have parts of me ... hopefully only the good parts. Would I go back and change certain things if I could? Perhaps ... but I could not expect any better members of humanity than I have been blessed to raise.

I don't want them to get too swollen of an ego, so here are a few more facts about them. Shelley had the incredible idea of buttering her bread BEFORE inserting it in the toaster. It took a while to figure out where that greasy mess was coming from. Will used to always fall out of bed and then roll underneath to sleep the rest of the night. Elizabeth once painted my lawnmower pure white without my permission and then denied it. Never let Shelley put away groceries if you hope to find them again. She also eats her pizza upside down. Elizabeth likes hot sauce and ranch on EVERYTHING. She can play guitar wonderfully but still expects me to tune it for her. Will does not like beans or broccoli or salads or peppers or tomatoes or just about any vegetable, but he loves beets ... go figure ... who the heck likes beets?

👍

Needed

The basement in my home consists of one large living area, probably 30ft x 20ft, and then four bedrooms. Over the past few years, this area had pretty much been taken over by teenagers and left as their hangout area. It is equipped with a big TV and ping pong table, a basketball game, a dartboard, a computer, a drum set, a sofa, a loveseat and a fireplace. It was their own space, often a mess, but a good area to call their own. Well, with kids heading out the door left and right as they begin to form their own lives, I have started to reclaim the basement and make it more homey again. There is a beautiful stone bar and fireplace down there and six large windows looking out at a private backyard surrounded by a woods. It is a great place to light a big fire in the Winter and watch the snow fall.

The ping pong table has been the location of a lot of laughter as well as fierce battles over the years. It has provided countless hours of fun. And just about every kid that has come along over the years has tried out the drum set. I am sure any neighbors within about a mile radius have enjoyed that. The basketball game is going to have to go. It is not working anymore. It was like those you see in an arcade with two hoops and a scoreboard to do battle against your opponent and the clock, but it no longer keeps score. The fireplace has been great in the winter. Get a good fire going in the morning and it makes the whole house feel warmer all day.

I am looking forward to what this area will look like when I am finished with painting and flooring and rearranging etc. … But I am afraid it will still feel a bit empty without all the kids running around. One day you are like the greatest person in the whole world to them and responsible for their every need. The next moment they are grown up and gone. It really happens fast and after you care for someone for so many years, it leaves a big hole when they no longer need you on a daily basis. You continue to love them and be proud of them every day, but life changes. I cannot complain. My life is very good compared to many. But I do miss those days when I was needed to make cocoa wheats and fix bicycles and sing silly songs.

What's For Dinner?

I have done a lot of Interstate traveling in my time and I have enjoyed seeing the variety that is America. On a recent trek down the highway though, I came to the realization that our food choices while traveling are sorely lacking. Those signs before each exit advertising the local choices all begin to look alike. There are about 10 different national chains that make up 99% of those sign advertisers and 9 of those 10 serve hamburgers.

Now I do enjoy a good hamburger every now and then, but is that all that traveling people are ever expected to eat? You say it's cheap and it's easy to eat on the road. Well, so is a chicken sandwich or a ham salad sandwich. What about a good hot dog? The "All American" hot dog is nowhere to be found along the highways of America.

What the heck is a vegetarian trucker to do? You say there aren't any? Well that is probably true. They all starved to death.

For Guys Only

Guys … yes this posting is for the guys only. If you are not a guy do not read this entry. Again, if you are female, read no further than the period at the end of this sentence.

OK guys, I am here to discuss some issues we need to fix with women. First of all, we need to find a way to make them follow instructions better. They always think they should just go ahead and do things their own way … like the ones who are still reading this after I already made it clear that they should not.

We need to train them to leave the toilet seat up at all times. There is no rule saying it needs to stay down just because she fell in the other night. I also wish women would realize that the turn signal in a car is NOT a ponytail holder. And that the rearview mirror is NOT a makeup mirror. It is a safety device.

Also we need to put our foot down and let our women know that the Mancave is forbidden territory when dumping their junk. You know how they like to throw their crap out there and then complain to you that it is a mess. And they throw it right in the middle of the floor. Would they like it if we put our junk in the middle of the hallway leading to the bathroom?

One last thing. Be very cautious when she says she wants to have a yard sale. It is just their sneaky way of getting rid of OUR things. I have three car battery chargers for a good reason. There is no need to sell any of them at a yard sale.

Oh, and one very last thing. NEVER, and I mean NEVER, let her talk you into going shopping for new flooring when the football game is on. It is just a power thing for her. That same store will be open all day tomorrow.

—

I was traveling. I exited the interstate to get some gas. I saw a Dairy Queen. I thought , "Hey, a milkshake sounds good!" I went inside to order.

The older woman at the register said, "Would you like free whipped cream and cherries on that?"

I replied, "No cherries."

She stared at me quite seriously and said, " I don't have a button for that."

—

Don't Miss Fall

A few weeks ago the weather made a sudden change around here from highs of a hundred to highs in the seventies. For me that change felt glorious. I love the comfortable warmth and the open windows on the house. The entire month of September was a nice mild time for weather. I have thoroughly enjoyed it.

Today is October 1st. Last night a cooler than usual breeze was blowing. This morning I awoke to a chilly crisp air. I donned a pair of sweatpants (my first of the season) and a sweatshirt and stepped outside. It felt like the first time in months that my lungs fully filled with the air. Nothing but the sweet crispness of Fall. It is sunny and will warm into a near perfect upper sixties this afternoon. I would take days like this year round. I feel more alive this time of year. I feel renewed.

Some people say that it only reminds them of what is coming. Winter will have its turn, but take the time to stop and enjoy the Fall. Soon leaves will turn into fabulous colors and you will even be able to light a fire in the evening and enjoy its warmth. I am looking forward to some warm apple cider and marshmallows roasting and kids coming around dressed in funny costumes looking for treats. Fall is in full swing. Don't miss enjoying a single day of it.

Wish Book

October is a great month for many reasons. The great weather, the beautiful leaves, the Fall festivals, pumpkin pie begins to reappear, football games, baseball playoffs, I get to pull my sweatpants out of storage. I could go on and on. The one thing that is missing though is the Wish Book.

The Sears Wish Book used to magically arrive in my house every year about this time. I would get my exercise running back and forth between mom and dad showing them all of the cool stuff I just had to have for Christmas this year. That book was always full of everything a kid could possibly want. Yes, they did waste the first half of the book on clothes and junk for those boring kinds of people, but the back half was loaded with all of the latest, coolest stuff to play with. Everything you could ever need all in one catalog.

When mom would sit down with me to look, I was always required to sit through 5 minutes of looking at pants and shirts, but then it would be my turn to show her the Evel Knevel Stunt Set and the Rock'Em Sock'Em Robots. With my selling skills she surely could see the value in these items. Dad was more fun. He would sit with me and look at the musical instruments and sporting goods. He did not feel the need to bore me with those pages of bedspreads and shoes. By the time December came along, that book would be worn out and I would have its pages memorized.

I learned a lot from that catalog. I would read about all sorts of things within its pages. I have not seen a Wish Book in years. I am not sure if they even still have it, but I know I sure miss it.

Advice for Women

I have been thinking about the habits of women recently. They do some funny things when you get to examining the subject. There are things they seem to have in common as a group. What got me to thinking about this was when I noticed that most women use the car turn signal as a ponytail holder repository. Do men with ponytails do this too? I then began to notice other unique habits of women. Women carry purses, but not in stores. When in stores they put their purse in the shopping cart and then make their husband push it around. Check for yourself, it's true!

I also have a couple of bulletins for women after my in depth study of this matter. Fake eyelashes. Why do some women wear these? Because, as a guy, I can tell you that it makes you look like you are ... well ... like you are wearing fake eyelashes or like you drove to work with your head hanging out the window and had a head-on collision with a wooly worm. It is NOT an appealing look.

Tying a jacket around your waist. Now I will admit that there are rare instances where this makes sense. For instance, you are going to a Friday night high school football game and it may get chilly after dark and you are gonna be out there for a few hours. But ladies, most of the time when I see you wearing this fashion disaster, this is not the case. You may think the world is fooled into thinking you may be cold later, but the truth is that it screams out to the world that you think your butt is too big. But trust me on this, covering your butt with a bulky jacket just makes it look bigger. And in all honesty, most of the time if you just left that jacket in the car, your butt is not that big anyhow. Besides, even if it is too big, the jacket just draws attention to the problem.

You are welcome ladies! I am glad I was here to help.

Will Cred

I am blessed with three incredibly intelligent children. They all have great potential in life. Sure, they do some quirky things from time to time, but they each are very capable. Shelley is especially capable in how she cares about the world and in her running marathons. She can make a major commitment and stick to it. That is a rare gift. Elizabeth has the gift of creativity. She expresses this best through her music. Will is an expert in technology and gaming. He can make sense out of many complex technical situations ... well at least I thought so until yesterday. Now, don't get me wrong, Shelley has about a 3.2 avg. in her junior year of college, Elizabeth just started college and has two A's on her first two tests and Will has about a 3.5 gpa in his high school junior year, although I now have my doubts about him.

You see, Elizabeth sent me a text from her college some 300 miles away yester day. It said "I got a 98 % on my test!" I was very proud and replied telling her so. To be inspirational, I forwarded the message to Will. Two minutes later I received a reply. "Yay! That's great! But why do you have dad's phone?"

Will just lost all his cred with me as a techno genius!

Vacation is Over

I have 14,000 things that need done today. I need to move some stuff around in the Mancave to make temporary room for some stuff belonging to a family friend who is soon moving from one place to another. I need to go get a spark plug for the chainsaw. I need to do some paperwork that I have been putting off. I need to mow the grass. I need to ship off something I sold on Ebay. I need to call the water company to get my account number because I cant find the bill. I need to repair the bad place in the front walk.

It is currently 11:49am. What have I accomplished so far? Well, I am writing this and I watched a James Bond movie on TV. That's right. I am lazy today. Oh , I will get in gear soon and get some stuff done, but I took this morning off from life. A little mini vacation and it felt good. So now it is time to get busy ... Well, right after breakfast of course. I think there is a box of Captain Crunch up there ... hey, give me a break, I am still on vacation until breakfast is over.

Chill Bumps

This time of year can create one of my favorite moments in life. It is a rare thing but it feels soooo good! This morning it was chilly outside. I hopped into my old Jeep and started up the road. About two miles into my trip the engine had warmed enough for me to have heat. With great anticipation I aimed the vents in my direction and turned it on low just long enough to evacuate any cold air remaining in the system. I then cranked it up to high and felt that oh so glorious chill run up my spine. That ticklish feeling that runs all the way up to the top of your head.

What the heck is that feeling anyway? And why can't I just do that any time I want? I absolutely love the sensation, but it is so rare. There are other things that will cause it from time to time, but my Jeep heater on a chilly morning can do it every time. I sure hope it's chilly tomorrow morning again!

Fall Break

Elizabeth is coming home from college for the weekend. She will arrive late tonight and return to school early Monday morning. She has me on her schedule for visitation between noon and 6pm on Saturday. The rest of her time is allotted for friend visitation. She has also requested spaghetti for lunch Saturday. She has always been my socialite child. She has tons of friends, several hundreds of Facebook friends and phone contacts. She rarely sits still and is always drinking fully from life's cup.

Will is on his Fall break from high school. He is the direct opposite, a homebody. He is spending his weekend getting to know his new robotic dinosaur. He saved his paychecks from work to buy this critter and finally it arrived yesterday. For what it cost him, I hope it can learn to wash the dishes or something.

Busy Busy Day

It was 36 degrees this morning when I got up at about 8am. A chilly start to the day. It is supposed to be in the mid-sixties with abundant sunshine this afternoon. I love days like this. I have lots of stuff I will get accomplished. I am going to repair the sidewalk. There is a place on the edge of one of the stones that is wearing away for some reason. I also need to mow the grass for hopefully the last time this year. I need to take a long nap. The little bottom strip on the garage door needs fixing as well. I need to run by the store and pick up some cat food. Their bowl is low and they are pacing with worried looks on their faces. I need to watch that one college football game this afternoon. That one cabinet door in the kitchen is kinda wiggly again.

Ok. So now I have my list. Now let me make my schedule for the day. The time is now 10:50 … so by the time I get this written it will be 11:00. Lunchtime! For lunch I can run over to that place with the German sausages. I love their Weiswurst and tater salad. I will get over there and finish eating by 12. I may as well go pick up the cat food while I am out. So run by the store, pick up some cat food and human food and home by 1:00 …

isn't that the time that ballgame starts? Ok, so I will watch the ballgame til 4:00 … late afternoon. I really wanted an afternoon nap today. Ok. Nap from 4 til 5. 5:00 to 5:15 look for screwdriver to fix that cabinet door. 5:15 to 5:16 tighten screws. 5:16 to 5:30 stand in kitchen and admire my handiwork. 5:30 to 6:00 return screwdriver to Mancave and get distracted by some cool stuff I bought at a yard sale a while back but haven't had time to mess with. 6:00 It's Dinnertime! 6:00 to 7:00 cook and eat dinner. 7:00 realize it is now dark outside and rest of chores will have to wait til another day.

But I did get MORE THAN HALF of my list completed today! I am a success!

—

These days people have all sorts of telephone ringtones. It is almost like a style statement for some. It is certainly a little piece of expressiveness. It sends a message to those around you.

Well, today I happened to be in a public restroom. There were approximately four other men in there as well. Everybody was simply going about their own business. Then it happened. From a closed stall over in the corner, there were suddenly the sounds of Donna Summer, the Queen of Disco, "Lookin' for some Hot Stuff baby this evening. Gotta have some Hot Stuff baby tonight!" I think that's enough said.

Don't Forget to Play

I turned 49 on Monday. I am now halfway to 98! My brother called and left a message offering to make me some reservations with the funeral director. My friends were all quick to point out that my next birthday is the big 50. My kids all reminded me of how ancient someone my age appears to them. What was my main birthday gift? A new basketball goal and ball. Then we all played HORSE. Who won? That's right! The old man kicked butt!

You see, I may be 49 on the outside, but on the inside I am still 10! I have been out there in the driveway every day this week playing, if only for a few minutes. I refuse to ever completely grow up.

I see too many adults who never take part in activities they see as being for kids. I say loosen up! Don't let the kids have all of the fun! In recent months I have gone bike riding and roller skating, played Frisbee, had a walnut fight with three kids in the backyard ... The list goes on and on. Don't be afraid to get out there and play.

I get it from my parents. My dad at age 86 went literally running through the woods with my kids carrying his cane in front of him. I also recall my mom riding the big rides at an amusement park in her later seventies. So get your butt out there today and play a little bit. It'll do you a world of good!

Occupy

This whole occupy Wall Street movement has been interesting for me to observe. These people are mad about the amount of money the top few percent of Americans have while others struggle to make ends meet. I was flipping through the radio stations when I came across a talk show host saying that he could not see anything valid for these protestors to complain about. Maybe I can clarify things for him a bit from my perspective as just some dummy in the crowd.

I have seen reports in recent years of top executives making massive bonuses and being paid out millions in severance pay even while their companies and investors were losing huge amounts of money. Explain to me the logic of how these people earned that payment. In some cases it was a buyout of a contract. Let's say this was a bank, does a teller who leaves their job with the bank get a contract buyout too? No, the teller was never given the option of negotiating the terms of their employment.

This radio guy said these executives worked hard to earn their money. Well, I would like to introduce Mr. Radio Guy to my trash collector. This man often works alone handling trash for more houses than you could imagine in a day. He works for a large company. I would guarantee you that the CEO does not work nearly as hard as my trash guy, yet I bet the CEO makes more in one year than my trash guy will make in a lifetime.

Now let's look at another side of this situation. My trash guy probably wants to buy a house someday or maybe he already has one. You can rest assured he could never afford to pay cash for it. Let's say he bought a house for sale for $150,000. Now that CEO could easily buy that house for $150,000 cash. Of course being a CEO let's say he buys a $300,000 house cash. In either case, he will still spend less money for his house than my garbage collector with a 30 year mortgage at 5.5%. His $150,000 house will cost him $306,606. And that is before the mortgage insurance he will be required to buy for the first few years. This same problem will often apply to cars and other major purchases. The poorer guy will often pay more for the same stuff.

The basics of life such as food and clothing etc. ... are all on a fairly even scale for everyone. You can choose the amount you wish to spend on those items based upon your budget and your tastes.

So what costs more for the CEO? Taxes.

I believe the issues that these protestors are fighting for is that some of the wealthiest make enough in a year to provide for necessities for the next few hundred years while others can work and not have enough to even meet all of their basic needs. Some rich executives do work very hard, but so do some very poor common laborers. Let's just stop the greed and find some compassion and common ground.

Haircut

I went to get a haircut the other day. I kind of enjoy the experience. It feels good to sit there and have someone messing around in your hair. The place I go has multiple people working there and I am not picky about which one does my hair. When they ask how I want it cut, I just tell them to make me beautiful. Their usual look is something akin to "God! I am just a hairdresser, not a miracle worker!" They will then proceed to cut my hair using scissors and clippers and shave my neck. A few years ago they also started trimming the hair in my ears. But on this most recent appointment, the girl who was doing my hair truly hurt my feelings when she said, "Do you want me to trim your eyebrows?"

My eyebrows don't look bushy do they? Only old men have bushy eyebrows! My grandfather had bushy eyebrows, not me! Young strong men like me never have bushy eyebrows! I am never letting that girl cut my hair ever again!

Made in Thailand

I enjoy specialty or unique grocery stores. You cannot buy everything in them, but you can usually find good quality and better variety than at the traditional places. I stopped by one of my favorites today to pick up a few things for dinner. I got some garlic seasoned potatoes, some fire roasted corn, and some salmon burgers. Dinner was great. Every morsel was consumed. No leftovers to put away.

I frequently will check the packaging of the food I buy for nutrition information and ingredients etc. ... I checked the salmon package and the only ingredient was wild caught salmon from the USA. Hey that sounded great to me! Below this it said processed in Thailand. ??? Product of Thailand. ???

So we caught this fish in the USA, exported it to Thailand to be processed and packaged, then imported it for sale in Indiana? Were we unable to freeze and box it here? Was it cheaper to send it on TWO boat trips across the Pacific than to pay someone here to do it? I am sooo confused.

Adult Timeout

Why do some people become so negative in life? So miserable with themselves that they even have to be mean and hurtful to others around them. It's almost as if they gain pleasure from causing others to join them in their misery. I have known people who are just always looking at the down side of things and never seem to allow themselves a happy moment. I also have known others who have been mean simply as a form of paybacks for perceived wrongdoings against them. It is sad in a life so brief that there are those who invest such time and energy into negative things. I witnessed one such person today.

I was shopping in a retail store and there was a woman at the customer service counter who had a very grimaced look on her face. As I waited behind her I could tell she was not in a great mood. The girl behind the counter finished with the customer she was waiting on. She then greeted this woman.

"How may I assist you?, the girl asked.

"It's about time you got some more help around here!", the woman snapped back. "I need to pick up my order". She then threw the receipt at the girl.

The girl looked up something on the computer and then got on the phone and called someone. "They will be right up with your order as soon as they are finished loading another order they are working on right now", the girl said with a smile.

"Well I don't have time to wait! This is ridiculous! I want somebody to get my stuff now so I can get out of here!"

The girl apologized and tried to be pleasant but to no avail. Finally, seeing that she was in a losing battle, she simply abandoned her station and everyone else waiting in order to go back and retrieve the order herself. This actually was making everyone else in line wait longer.

The woman had gotten exactly what she wanted yet she still looked mad at the world. Being the ornery old fool that I am, I could not let this moment pass. I looked this woman straight in the eye and I smiled great big.

"Isn't this a beautiful day outside?", I said.

She looked at me like I was some kind of nut.

" I love coming here to shop. There are so many different stores I could go to, but the people at this store are always so friendly. Don't you think so?" I continued. " I think maybe I should bring them some boxes of doughnuts the next time I come just to show my appreciation."

She was now positive I was a nutcase.

I then just stood there and smiled at her quietly.

Shortly thereafter the girl returned with a large box and the woman was on her way without another word.

Why did she feel the need to be like that? I will never understand. That girl behind the counter was just doing her job trying to earn a paycheck. She had nothing to do with that woman's misery, yet she caught the most of the wrath.

Maybe we need to institute time-outs for adults.

Make it the Best

It's the night before Thanksgiving and all through the house the children are stirring in anticipation of the feast to come. This is the traditional start of the holiday season. All sorts of fun things begin now. From the preparation for tomorrow's meal, to the family gatherings and holiday parties, the exchanging of cards and gifts, and the renewed sense of family and love. It can be a great 6 weeks.

For some, however, it can be a time of great misery. Reminders of broken families and lost loved ones, of failed relationships and of financial woes. Being alone and poor at this time of year can make things not so merry. The world is too materialistic, and for those who struggle just to pay the electric bill each month, the holidays are quite stressful.

There is nothing at all wrong with being alone on a holiday if it is by choice or circumstance and you still feel loved and a part of a family. It happens. But the people I feel sorry for are the ones who are simply alone in this world for whatever the reason and don't feel like they are a part of something.

Sit down and think about it. You probably know somebody who would be thoroughly touched by a plate of turkey or some holiday cookies or an invitation to go shopping together or just an afternoon visit. It will mean the world to them and probably do you a lot of good as well. The holiday season can be whatever you make it to be, about things, or about people.

The Shopping News

It's Black Friday. I just ate my breakfast. Turkey and taters and a small piece of ham. Millions of people are out pushing and shoving their way through stores looking for bargains. Many more are working to service all of these shoppers. Those retail workers have a trying job putting up with working when everyone else is off and dealing with all too frequently rude and overly demanding consumers. Be nice to those people who are working to make your shopping easier. It is not their fault you had to stand in line for 15 minutes to check out. If they had called in sick, your wait would have been even longer. Show them some love.

I read this morning about some woman in California who did not show the love. She pepper sprayed other shoppers to keep them away from the stuff she wanted. Was that new TV really worth it? Is that what Christmas is all about?

Now back to my breakfast. I love turkey. I always have. The cats are all happy too. They have been all giddy knowing there are turkey scraps in the house. And why did I have taters for breakfast? Because day old taters are the best! They develop a whole nuther layer of flavor with time. Speaking of time, I recently bought some 1000 day aged Gouda cheese at the store. I ate some of it this morning too. It is awesomely strong. Something you either love or hate. It is a good, stinky cheese.

I like extended weekends like this. I don't have a lot on my agenda. I should be able to tinker on some things. I need to clean leaves from gutters and pile up some branches I trimmed from trees around the yard. There are always a dozen things that need fixing around the house and I can usually find a football game or two on TV. Shopping? No, no thanks. I will do that on a weekday in early December when the stores are quiet and slow.

Motorcycle Guy

Hey motorcycle guy! Yes, you! The one who was riding down the interstate in busy traffic with no helmet and popping wheelies. Yes, you! What in the world were you thinking? You want to pop wheelies? That's fine, go for it! But on a busy interstate with 6 lanes of traffic going in one direction? Next to semi trucks? What were you thinking? Were you trying to be noticed? Did you want people to see you? To comment on your talents? Well, we all saw you. We all commented on you. I think the most common word used by witnesses to your act was IDIOT! Was it really worth it? That one wheelie you did was shaky at best. You came close to losing it. You were doing about 60mph. There was a semi on your left and a 10 ft high cement wall on your right. Which direction were you planning on rolling? I was just curious. I would not have been the one having to scrape up what was left of you or to go tell your family what happened. I would have just felt sorry for you. The truth is that I already do. I hope you can figure it out before it is too late.

Doing it Right

Life is all about gains and losses, successes and failures and what we can retain from those experiences. We all do some things right and we all make mistakes. Sometimes we know what we are doing at the time is wrong, sometimes we thought it seemed like the best idea at the moment. Sometimes we are given credit for things we do not deserve, sometimes we are convicted for things we never did. We gain friendships and relationships along the way due to circumstance or chance, we lose relationships along the way due to reasons too numerous to mention. But the grand total of these things equals our life.

I wish we were able to inventory our lives for the important stuff more often than we do. We get so caught up in the manmade experience of jobs and status and materialism and self importance that we often fail to nurture the things that matter most. We assume that our relationships are all fine. We take them for granted. Then all of the sudden, it's too late. You suddenly miss what it was that person had to offer that you so cherished in your life. It is just gone. You are left with a hole in your being that never really heals.

We can all do a better job at being good to one another. We should all make that a priority every day. We should strive to always say and do things that are right and just and good. Because in the long run doing anything but the right thing really makes very little sense.

Feeling Fee

Yesterday was a day for paying bills. This chore is something that makes me sad as I give away all of my money for various services rendered. I bought another plank or two of my house and gave the bank a lot of money in the form of an interest payment for the privilege. I did the same with the car. I also paid the cable and phone bills. Those two, along with gas, electric, and water these days now charge a convenience fee for taking my money. Now just who is this convenient for? Certainly not me! Go ahead and inconvenience me by making me continue to carry that money around in my pocket!

I hear people say, "That's just the way it is." when talking about things like this. "How are you going to fight a big company?" Well, I know for a fact that the "company" did not make the decision to fleece my pocket a little more. Someone or a group of someones who works at that company did that. Why do we never see those individuals on the TV news being grilled with questions about how they thought it was a good idea to have people pay for the right to give them more money?

I think I should be able to charge these companies I do business with a convenience fee for sending my money to them rather than making them chase me down for it. I am certainly making their job easier. If it is such an inconvenience for me to call you up and give you money, so much so that you feel the need to charge me extra, then maybe I actually should stop doing that. I should make you drop by the house and pick up your money. Would that be more convenient for you?

More and more people at these companies are finding ways to charge us fees for spending our own money. I am beginning to miss the good old days of cash.

Experience the Holidays

There is a lot of Christmasing starting to go on around town. Trees are flying out the door at the local hardware store and colorful lights are appearing on rooftops and fences throughout the neighborhood. Stores are busy with people who have a sort of stressful joy on their faces. Diets are being abandoned until the new year. And children seem to be just a bit more hyper each and every day.

There is a good side to the season. It's not the buying frenzy or the perfectly decorated house or the travel stress. The good side is in much more important things. People tend to give more of themselves this time of year either through volunteering or donating time or money. They even trade smiles with perfect strangers more. Those are all good things. There is also the extended time spent with loved ones that seems to occur. Those times are so precious and need to be cherished. There is also the reminiscing of holiday seasons past and of the loved ones we were blessed to share those times with who are no longer with us. Of course we miss them, but we should also smile in our hearts at the memories we made together.

There are the simple pleasures of the season. Grandma's homemade cookies and peanut butter balls and nut rolls. There is the great escape of sitting down one night and watching Charlie Brown or Rudolph while sipping hot cider and feeling like you are 7 years old once again. It's a great feeling to allow yourself to indulge in such simple pleasures.

We also help in creating those types of memories for others around us. Just the other day my son, Will, reminded me that it was about time for me to make a batch of sausage cheese balls. That is one of the little things that means Christmas to him. I also think that he is hoping that I will make them before Elizabeth gets home from college for holiday break. I recall one year where Elizabeth and her friend Michelle were sitting in the kitchen eating sausage balls just as fast as I could pull them out of the oven. Then they would sit there waiting for the next batch with unwavering enthusiasm. The other kids in the house hardly had a chance. We also always make Chex mix and chocolate covered pretzels this time of year and homemade pizza on Christmas Eve. My daughter, Shelly, has always been the biggest fan of my homemade pizza. Just cheese, no meat, and lots of sauce.

I have many good memories from this time of year. One year we knew of a struggling family, so on December 24th, we left a bunch of presents on their doorstep. That was one of the best feelings in the world to secretly brighten someone's day. We never said a word about it and I am certain those people wonder to this day where that stuff came from.

My dad was always filled with Christmas spirit. He would bounce around the house singing Christmas songs and decorating all of the doorways and windows. He loved to give.

My funniest Christmas memory involves a tree. I had a girl-friend who wanted a real tree. I wanted to find the perfect one for her. Curt and I went out early one morning and chopped it down, threw it on the car and delivered it to my girlfriend. I hope those people who owned that property did not miss their tree too much.

So as you move into this holiday season, take little moments to savor its blessings. Don't get all caught up in the unimportant stuff. For example, I am certain that there was some gift that I felt I just had to have for Christmas in 1977 or 1978 or 1982 or whatever year. Do I remember what those things were? Well, maybe one or two of them. The rest of the years I have no clue. What I ended up cherishing in my memories is the little things I often took for granted … my dad playing "Here comes Santa Claus" on the guitar, old Mrs. Bannon's nut bread, going ice skating on the cow pond up the road, those lifesavers storybooks filled with candy, traveling all over the countryside delivering cookies with my mother to old people and shut-ins. Those are my best experiences.

Diets

I watched part of a show on PBS yesterday about the Mayo Clinic Diet. It was full of common sense stuff. Control portion size, eat lots of fresh vegetables and fruit, eat more fish and less red meat, eat whole grains. We all know this stuff. We all want to be as healthy as we can be. Yet, when I drive by these fast food joints, they are packed with people loading up on the high fat, low nutritional quality stuff. Why do we always seem to work against ourselves?

If you were to ask the average person to write down all of the foods they like, the list would almost always include some sort of fresh fruit or vegetable, yet how often do we eat potato chips or cheese curls instead? I can sit there and eat a chili dog knowing full well that I should have had the baked fish I love and I will feel guilty later, but in that moment, that chili dog is all I can think about. Why are we wired like that? Shouldn't we crave the stuff we need instead?

Also, when it comes to junk, we can absolutely gorge ourselves. We can eat and eat and eat pizza and fried chicken wings, but have you ever heard someone say, "If I eat one more carrot, I think I will burst!" I can recall eating my way into misery a few times in life, but it never seems to have involved healthy food.

Things that are high in fats and preservatives and calories seem to now dominate our diets. I personally love many foods that are good for me, but many of them rarely find their way to my plate. Why? First of all, they are often less convenient to prepare. Secondly, they are harder to find in the grocery store.

The other issue is as our lives become more automated, we expend less energy. Therefore, we actually need fewer calories. We used to wash dishes by hand. Now we have a machine that does this. The same with our clothes. We used to burn many calories just keeping our bodies warm or cold. Now we live in temperature controlled environments. Kids used to go outside and play every day. Now most kids rarely venture out of the house other than to get into the car.

Anyhow, enough rambling. There are thousands of different diets out there, but the truth is that to maintain better health you simply need to eat a lot more of the good stuff and less of the bad. And get your butt up and moving every single day. Also, this cannot be a short term plan, but must be a permanent change for it to truly work. Think about what you are putting into your body and how much you are moving. It's that simple!

Ok, so why the pep talk? It's really for me. I feel fat and want to lose about 10 pounds. I lost 25 last winter but have gained back 15 of that. I hate the thought of giving up banana splits and 5 Guys burgers but I love it when I am more skinny and have more energy. So here are my basic weight loss rules. Drink water with every meal. Eat some raw stuff every day. Don't eat anything with ingredients I can't pronounce. Eat when I am hungry instead of when the clock says it's time to eat.

I guess I could print this and buy a TV ad and charge $14.95 plus shipping and handling for the info. What the heck is handling anyhow?

My Wish List

With one week of December already gone, I am sure that most of you have either already been Christmas shopping or else you intend to get started soon. I am also sure that you are anxiously awaiting my Christmas list so you will know what to get me this year. I am happy to supply you here and now with the list of things I hope to find under my tree this year.

1) A replacement knob for my Zoom R16. I lost it somewhere along the way and despite approximately 15 calls over the past 9 months to customer service, I still do not have this little 50 cent piece of plastic. 11 of my calls have produced nothing. The other 4 calls have produced a promptly sent part, always a different part, always the wrong part. At this pace, in another few years I will have a whole brand new unit ... minus that same darned knob I was missing in the first place.

2) Riding lessons for that unicycle I bought at a yard sale last spring. I am SO CLOSE! I can almost get it going. I can balance, but once I start to move, I am in trouble. Maybe you

should throw in some elbow pads, knee pads, a helmet, and a prepaid accidental health insurance policy.

3) Jane's grandma's chocolate cookies. Growing up, my neighbor, Jane, had a grandma who made these homemade soft chocolate sugar cookies. She would always seem to save a few for me. They were awesome, but I haven't had any in about 30 years.

4) Half a dozen Jimmie's Lunch dogs. I love hot dogs. I love chili dogs (what some people call Coney dogs) even more. Growing up I was blessed to live in an area with 2 excellent hot dog joints. One was named Shorty's and is still going strong. The other was called Jimmie's Lunch but it has been closed for a long time now. The two places were both great but just different. I get to have a Shorty dog sometimes, but I sure could use a Jimmie's.

5) An old pickup truck or cargo van. That way I could bring home more treasures from yard sales!

6) A new motor home and gas for a year. Hey, I may as well dream big!

7) An all expenses paid trip to the Buckwheat Festival in West Virginia. Buckwheat cakes and sausage galore. It doesn't get any better.

8) A Holideck. If you ever watched Star Trek you will understand.

Most of all I hope to reconnect with lost friends and loved ones. To receive an unexpected phone call or card. To find peace and tranquility in my heart and in the world.

It's Time

It's time! It's really time! It's time to make the first batch of Chex mix for the season. I make a big batch, place it in zip lock baggies and watch the kids inhale them. I might even eat one or two ... or three or four ... bags.

Also, Will has been asking me to make sausage ball before Elizabeth gets home from college to eat them all. I may work on a batch of those as well. The cats think that is just a way to ruin perfectly good sausage by covering it with that biscuit crap.

This time of year does make me miss something about my years in Tennessee. My work took me to many people's homes and this time of year I usually scored a few pounds of homemade sausage in those little burlap sacks. That was some good stuff. I should have added that to my Christmas list!

Working in homes this time of year meant I got to sample all sorts of good stuff. Everybody had their own traditions and favorites. That was a fun part of my job.

I haven't pestered mom about cookies and nut rolls yet this year. In recent years she has commented that it is getting harder to get this annual tradition accomplished. C'mon mom! You are only 86! Get up off your bum and get busy! I honestly feel she should have sent one batch right after Thanksgiving and then one about the 10th of December, followed by a final box arriving on the 23rd. Sounds reasonable to me!

I always try to make her homemade pizza recipe on Christmas Eve. It has become a tradition for my kids. It is a different kind of pizza with an awesome sauce and a few unusual tricks to it. I have sometimes thought about opening a pizza shop just to sell it to the masses.

I did go Christmas shopping for a little bit yesterday. I am intrigued by the fake price tags department stores put on items in an attempt to show value. I noticed one pair of gloves, nothing special, just gloves, which had a price tag of $54 on them. Of course they were on sale for a whopping 60% off! What a bargain, right? Except for the fact that these were about $15 gloves to begin with.

I also saw this motion activated dispenser for candy/gumballs/ m&m's etc. … It was kinda cool. I saw it in one store for $29.00. I saw the same machine in an upscale store for $49. Was it simply better based upon where I bought it? Interesting.

At the mall I go to there are two competing oriental restaurants in the food court. Each of them has a woman standing out in the walkway giving free chicken samples. On a busy day, if you just keep walking back and forth, you can get filled up in about 15 minutes for free and they will never even notice you. Some of the security guards at my mall have Segways. They stand there and ride around all day. I once encountered one of them in the parking lot in "pursuit" of a young gentleman. The guard never got off the Segway but just kept weaving and bobbing until he had chased the young perpetrator all the way across the parking lot and off of the property. The whole chase seemed like it took about 10 minutes but was entertaining to watch.

The mall is always a good place for people with "look at me" syndrome. Where the heck do they even find some of the stuff they be wearing? I saw one woman yesterday whose boots made it look like she had not shaved below her knees in at least a year or two. Is that supposed to be a desirable look? I also encountered this furry hat thing that had earflaps coming all the way down to form mittens at your waist. Are you kidding me?

I must admit that it is all a bit entertaining even if it is ridiculous.

By the Fireplace

I just lit a fire in the fireplace in the basement tonight. I am writing this while I wait for it to build up and warm up. It is a nice night for a fire, all crisp and cool outside, a few flurries in the air. I am thinking I will hang out down here tonight after dinner. It also looks like I will have some company as Fuzzbutt the cat is already over there checking out the progress of the fire. He absolutely loves to lay all stretched out on the ottoman when the fireplace is going.

I am having tater soup and cornbread for dinner tonight. It goes well with a fire. All I will need now is a blanket, a pillow and a good old fashioned Christmas show on TV and I will be set for the evening. I even have a jug of cider in the fridge. I may have to warm me some.

Get Happy

We fill our lives with human ambitions. We often admire or envy those who have something we do not. People are hooked on reality TV and celebrity and stardom and wealth and power. Why? It does not matter who you are. You are no more or less important than anybody else. Each one of us is simply made from a pile of dirt and water mixed together. We end up with different appearances and personalities, but we are all made from the same stuff. No royalty, no trash, just all the same.

It is also true that for each and every one of us being alive is nothing short of a miracle. When you look at everything that had to occur at precisely the right moment over the course of time for you to be standing here today, it is absolutely astonishing.

I believe we need to think more about our good fortunes and embrace what we have been given with a joyful heart. The anger and resentment and negativity in the world really have no place here. Nor does the "class ranking" and dog eat dog attitude. We should all just be ecstatic to be here each and every day and take that positive and share it with every other lucky soul who resides upon this earth with us.

Cereal

Cereal is a funny sort of food that almost everybody eats in one form or another. No matter what your age, almost everybody enjoys a bowl every now and then. I am sitting here right now enjoying some that was left over from when I made party mix the other day. Speaking of which, the party mix is almost gone too.

Anyhow, cereal comes in so many variations. I like hot cereals like cream of wheat and oatmeal. I guess you would call oatmeal a cereal. I also like Cocoa Wheats. That is some awesome stuff. For those of you who do not know what I am talking about, it is like chocolate Cream of Wheat. The reason I mention this is because in Tennessee, we could never find Cocoa Wheats in the store. But, Shelly loved them. So, every few months we would get in a fresh shipment from grandma. I also enjoy many cold cereals both healthy and unhealthy for you. I have always considered Cheerios to be one of my favorites. I also like Cap'n Crunch and Golden Grahams, just to name a couple. I also look for Boo Berry around Halloween. Yes, I admit it. I like a lot of cereals made for kids.

I have been frustrated for many years that I cannot recall the name of one of my all time favorite cereals as a kid. I am assuming it is no longer made as I have often searched the shelves of the grocery store for it. All I can recall is that is was a graham cereal that was shaped like wagon wheels. It looked similar to Honeycombs. I loved that stuff!

Pap, my grandfather, always ate bran cereals or shredded wheat. We always called that hay bale cereal. Also, my mom taught us to warm the milk before putting it on cereal. You should try it. It is really good that way! My dad once convinced me to eat my Cheerios with warm water and sugar on them. We lived way out in the country and I would bet we were out of milk, but he made it sound so cool that I gobbled them up like they were delicious.

I like the fact that cereal is versatile. It's breakfast food, a snack, or dinner. It can be warm, cold, crunchy or soggy. It's all in how you like it. You can even take it with you in the morning and eat it while you drive with your knee on your way to work. How cool is that?

Injured

My oldest daughter will be turning 21 later this week. My son, who is my youngest will be turning 17 next month. My best friend from childhood will be 50 next month. How did all of these people get so old so fast?

Personally, I am feeling like I am about 16. Some might say that I often act more like I am a 3 year old. I am glad I am not aging as fast as my children and my friend! Well, I guess I cannot say that about my 17 year old, Will. He is leaving childhood begrudgingly. He likes being a kid and I think that is great. There will be plenty of time for being an adult when the time comes. For now he enjoys his video games and the computer. Heck, I still enjoy the video games and computer myself.

As for me, my body does not always cooperate with the assumption that I am still 16. It can send me a harsh message to the contrary when I forget how old I really am and try to do something silly. Just the other day I was sitting on the arm of the sofa for a minute watching something on TV. When I got up to go to the kitchen I somehow tripped over my own foot and fell flat on my face. Who left that foot laying there anyway?

I was out shooting basketball the other day in the driveway. You should see me. I have an awesome six inch vertical these days! Anyhow I took a shot and it bounced off the rim to the left. As I raced at a blinding speed to catch up to it, I accidentally collided shin first with Elizabeth's car. My leg was purple for a week. Don't tell Elizabeth what happened or she will be worried about ... the car. All I can say is that she should have parked it elsewhere before going back to college.

Seeing the Lights

Do you know what time it is? This weekend is the prime time to pile the family in the car and hit the road. Where are we going? Oh, not far! It is time to load up the car, turn the radio to a station playing Christmas music, and drive around the neighborhood looking at the lights. Some of our neighbors put a lot of work into creating this free entertainment for us. It is our job to get out there and enjoy it! The kids may protest at first as you drag them away from the Playstation, but before the night is over they will enjoy this trip or else! You may have to bribe them with a stop for drinks or even dinner, but it is our job as parents to force them to enjoy this annual outing even if it kills them! Most kids will fall into the spirit of things once you get on the road and they will actually end up enjoying the trip. There will, however, always be the diehard teen who wants to prove a point by acting miserable the whole trip. All you have to do for them is take their cell phone and tell them they will not get it back until they start looking at the lights and looking happy about it.

"I said smile dammit! That's not a smile! I need to see some teeth!"

As a last resort, you can always threaten to read all of the text messages on their phone aloud to the whole family in the car. No kid can risk that sort of humiliation.

The Mall in December

The weather outside is not frightful and I don't have a delightful fire lit because it's too warm out for that and there is no snow to speak of in the forecast. Hard to believe its only 4 days til Christmas.

I will tell you the one thing that is very frightful these days. A trip to the mall! Those people there are not like normal people I see other places the rest of the year. Where do they live anyhow? Where do they work? Even more importantly, how do they work in those clothes? I saw one woman there tonight whose boots were so tall they almost qualified as pants! They were like fashionable hip waders. There was also a man with these funny looking earmuffs on. Why was he wearing them inside? The sales clerk in one of the stores had a bunch of tattoos and piercings. She also had a splint on her finger. I wanted to ask her if it was from a tattooing accident, but she looked a lot meaner than me.

I am always entertained by the girls who work at the stand in the middle of the mall who stalk women with bad hair offering to straighten HALF of their hair for free! Then there is the place where they give massages right out in the middle too. I could never find it relaxing to get a massage while a million people raced by in a shopping frenzy.

I don't particularly enjoy shopping at the mall, but sometimes people's Christmas wish lists force me to brave the crowd. It's just a fact of life.

Forward With Hope

Whatever Christmas means to you, I hope it has been a good one. It is currently 10 pm on Christmas day and I have done about all of the Christmasing I can do. It was a good day in many respects, yet quite empty in others. The loved ones who were missing created a hole inside of me that nothing can fill. We all are missing someone when Christmas rolls around. Someone who is no longer or not currently with us for one reason or another. The best thing to do is to cherish the ones who are still here, for one day they may also be gone, and you don't want to miss a moment with them either.

Life will never stop throwing you new challenges and unexpected change. You simply must find a way to keep moving forward, to be the best you can be, and to somehow offer the world something of true value in the kind of person that you are. The definition of being human should always include the fact that we are not perfect, but we should always strive to be better humans in the way we treat others and ourselves. It is sometimes difficult to look beyond pride or insecurity or self reward to see the better choices we should all be making. I believe that it is how we each respond to the results of our shortcomings that is truly the measure of the person inside each of us.

This period between Christmas and New Years is a great time for reflection not only upon the ending year, but on our lives as a whole. May we make good use of this opportunity to become even better in the coming year.

—

I am here today to make a public admission. I have been unfaithful. It all happened so innocently. I stopped by her house for just a few minutes. She had beautiful blonde hair and such a loving personality. I just could not resist. She was so easy to like and she seemed to genuinely enjoy my company as well. Yes, I admit it. I petted another cat today and Fuzzbutt is not one bit happy about it!

Looking Ahead

From age nine to age twenty-nine I played drums in a band somewhere every single New Year's Eve. Since age thirty, I have always been home on the big night. Tonight will be no different. I feel I have seen a lot in those twenty straight years I was out amongst the masses. All sorts of unusual human behavior. Now I like to treat this night as a quiet night of personal reflection on what has come to pass and as a chance to evaluate my plans for the future. I currently feel very positive about my future. I have a lot of good things going on. Just as with my past, I am certain there will be great positives as well as failures. Hey, that's life. We can become better humans from all of our experiences.

The big thing we each always need to have is new challenges. The chance to work on a fresh set of opportunities. To be inspired by a new road to travel is never a bad thing.

I am very curious where I will be in life at this time next year and I feel that is a good thing. I do feel sorry for those who already know the answer to that question. So as you think about your coming year, don't just settle. Reach out and dream a little. Strive to achieve things you may fear are not within your reach. Prove that doubt within yourself wrong. You may be surprised where you can end up. But it certainly won't hurt to try.

Oh My Back

I injured my back yesterday while acting like I was 12 years old. I get into trouble a lot that way these days. In my mind I am still a kid, but my body frequently reminds me otherwise. The result of yesterday's escapade is that today I cannot reach my left foot no matter how hard I may try. I also am walking in a sideways slanted position. Just about any movement hurts. If I find a comfortable position and stay there, then I am ok. The moment I decide to change positions, I am in trouble.

I did run up to see the chiropractor a while ago to see if she could help me. She worked me over and taped me up and said she would see me again tomorrow. She didn't really say how long it will take to heal me. She seemed preoccupied on the phone after my treatment ordering a new ski boat, so I didn't get the chance to ask her.

I am gonna go take a long, hot bath soon. That seems to ease my pain. The only problem is getting in and out of the tub. I may just stay in there and keep rewarming the water until tomorrow.

Fascinating People

I am always fascinated by people and their stories. I met a man today who lives in a quiet neighborhood on the outskirts of a small town. He was an older weathered looking fellow with a pleasant, yet crusty personality. He took great pride in telling me about the day when a stolen school bus being pursued by a massive line of police cars came barreling down his little street. He gave me all of the details about the spike strips they threw out to flatten the tires and how it brought quite a scare to the fellows down the road when they saw school bus headlights racing between the houses. He told me that other than that his neighborhood had been fairly quiet lately. I wonder with how many people he has shared that story. It was obviously a highlight in his memory.

I also visited a lady who had a picture of a village. Like many artifacts in a home, there was a story behind this picture. It was a gift from a friend from China. The picture, elaborate in detail, was made entirely of butterfly and grasshopper wings. I was truly amazed.

I spend a lot of time listening to the stories of others. It is something I enjoy making the time to do. If you ask the right questions, you can find all sorts of fascinating tidbits.

Itch

My leg keeps itching. I keep scratching and it keeps itching. There is nothing visible there. It just itches. What the heck is that all about? An itch is an odd sensation. It is a signal from your body saying, "Hey! You big dummy! Scratch here!" Animals do the exact same thing. How do we automatically know when something itches to scratch it? There are even many times when mothers say "I know it itches, but don't scratch it!" No wonder kids get confused. Their own body says scratch and their own mothers threaten to take away the TV if they do! What's a kid to do? And why would your body tell you to scratch if it was bad for you? I am sitting here scratching my head in confusion.

👍

Crazy Old Lady Not

I went to briefly visit a retired lady I know today. She claims to have a cat and even has a food bowl out for it in the kitchen, but I have never, ever seen it. She told me a story about an event last winter that probably has the neighbors wondering about her sanity as well.

It seems some squirrels had chewed into her telephone line that runs to the house. The weather was bad and snowy and repairmen were slow to respond. She wanted to let a couple of friends know that she was doing ok as she knew they would be worried about her with the bad weather and all. She does not own a cell phone, but she recalled that her car had OnStar installed in it. She knew she could make calls through the service but she wasn't 100% certain how it worked. Just to be safe, she started the car and backed it out into the driveway, leaving the engine running while she made her calls. She would sit in the driveway appearing to talk to herself to any passersby and then a few minutes later, she would pull her car back into the garage and go back in the house. This pattern continued for a few days at various times until the repairmen could get to her house to fix the line. She has since been informed that the OnStar will work just fine from inside the garage with the engine off. I feel reasonably certain that the neighbors will be relieved even if a bit less entertained.

The Debate

It is the season for political debates. The politicians are experts in saying a whole lot while saying nothing at all. They almost never give a straight answer to any question. They speak their own version of English. It involves a lot of ambiguity. I have an idea. Why don't we stage a debate sponsored by the American people? The questions would come from regular people and would not be pre-screened or given in advance to the candidates. Also, the questions would all be the type to which there would only be permitted a yes or no answer. If any candidate said more than yes or no they would be disqualified from the election. That would make them squirm!

I have some sample questions to get us started.

"Mr. Candidate, did you pay more than $50 for that haircut? $75? $150? Have you ever stepped inside a Great Clips?"

"Mrs. Candidate, have you ever lived more than six months without a maid or a nanny?"

"Mr. Candidate, should the Congress have better healthcare than the rest of us Americans?"

"Mr. Candidate, do you know what ramen noodles taste like?"

"Mr. Candidate, have you ever personally waited on hold for 20 minutes just to talk to a customer service rep at the cable company?"

"Mrs. Candidate, have you ever stood in a line at Wal-Mart at 7pm on a Saturday?

Those are just a few questions to get the party started.

Art Class

I was sitting in a large conference room today when I smelled something. Something familiar. Something from my past. I was immediately transported in my mind back to Mr. Halpern's Jr. High art class. Mr. Halpern has resided in that same classroom filled with all sorts of art supplies for a couple of decades before I came stumbling along one Fall morning. By that time the place already had its own character. And its own smells. The place did not smell bad at all, just different. All of that crayon and charcoal and paint had created a certain homeyness in the air. It was kinda relaxing.

Mr. Halpern understood that not all of us were budding Picassos. He simply allowed us to create whatever we set our minds to do in about an hour and then we turned it in each day for a grade. If he felt you had given your best effort, then you usually got a B. He had to save the A's for the real artists among us. There was a certain peace about that class. No big pressure to do anything fabulous except to create.

I will never be an artist, but I am happy I got to try. And I am happy that scent brought back the memories of those carefree hours of my youth.

—

It is YOUR life to live as YOU see fit.

Super Sunday

The Super Bowl is right down the street from my house this year. It would have been fun to go but the price is awfully steep. I went on EBay just to check. I found a pair in the 15th row on the 50 yard line for $29,000. I thought that might be a little beyond my budget. I then did a search for the lowest priced ones and StubHub had some for $2495 per ticket, but I think my house is closer to the action than those seats. I guess I will just have to watch from my living room again. The food is better and the atmosphere is still good. Parking isn't a major problem and the animals seem to enjoy sharing the sofa with me.

I cannot imagine spending thousands of dollars on 3 to 4 hours of entertainment unless it is gonna be awfully darned special. If I were to spend that on going to the Super Bowl, then the cheerleaders had better be giving me a foot massage and I need to have John Madden sitting next to me for my own personal play-by-play. I would need to be invited to hand over the trophy to the winners and join them for the celebration afterwards.

Oh well, I will have to struggle along at home with my cheese dip and nachos. I may even be able to sneak in a nap during the 3rd quarter.

This Speck

I have been thinking about life. Each of us just all of the sudden one day appears here on Earth, spends x number of years here, and then disappears back into the ground from which we came. They say the planet has been around for a few billion years. I have been here less than fifty. In another fifty, I will probably be gone again. Where the heck was I for those first few billion years? And more importantly to me now is where will I be for the next few billion years? Many people have many different answers to that question. Life is wonderful and rewarding in so many ways, but we spend a lot of our time worrying about what is going on within this speck of time in which we live.

People always speak of their beliefs about the future. What are their beliefs about our past? Did we each not exist prior to magically appearing here over this past century? Where the heck were we? We are each made up of all sorts of molecules. I wonder where my molecules have been. Was one of my molecules ever inside a dinosaur or on another planet or an asteroid? Did any of my molecules ever make something big happen? I am betting my molecules have seen a lot in their day.

I like to ponder stuff like that. I like to think of all of the possibilities about things I will never be able to figure out. I like the mystery in it all. It would be so cool to have the answers, but it may be even cooler just having the questions.

Talk about feeling small! I was reading today that scientists have finally found some planets similar in size to Earth. They are only like 900 light years away. They said the Space Shuttle would be able to get there in like 34 million years if it left today. Holy crap! This is one big universe we live in! And yet we spend our time worrying about so many petty things.

I wish I could live in the future and experience space travel. Put me on the USS Enterprise and send me to visit alien worlds. Just don't send me on a date with a Klingon woman. They are too mean for me.

I cannot begin to imagine what fascinating sights must be out there on all of those different planets. We really have no clue. We just blindly accept that we are here. We get so self involved that we often forget that we are each just a speck of dust on a speck of dust flying through space.

Anyhow, it is time for this speck of dust to go have dinner. Even a speck has to eat!